HEART OF THE COUNTRY

Professional hints & tips for colouring

1 Before you start

To colour up a drawing properly you need to be well prepared. Sit upright with a straight back and posture. Work in natural light or beneath a good light source, but not in direct sunlight. Choose a flat or slightly angled surface to work on. Remove a page from your book and secure it to your surface with tape to prevent it from slipping. You can use either traditional coloured pencils, any water-based paints, or colouring pencils that can be mixed with water to create watercolour effects. Keep a cloth and eraser handy in case you need to make any changes. You are now ready to start.

2 Applying colour

There are many ways to paint a picture – over time you will develop your own method. Taking the front cover image as an example, a good place to start is the background. Blues are 'cold' colours and drop back whereas reds and oranges are 'warm' colours and jump forward. Also, light shades drop back and darker shades come forward. You can research the colour of the main subjects and background details by referring to books and following the colours accurately, or you can make them up as you go. Use broader areas of colour for the background first and add the details of colour and shadow later. The foreground subjects should be darker and stronger than the background.

3 Finishing off

Once you have painted your picture, stand back and look to see if there are parts that need a bit more work and that it all comes together. It is sometimes better to 'under work' than 'over work' a picture as it may end up being 'muddy' and confused. Let your painting dry out and be careful not to smudge coloured pencils. Keep finished pictures stored safely in a flat folder. If you are pleased with the result, why not get it framed so that it can be admired by family and friends!

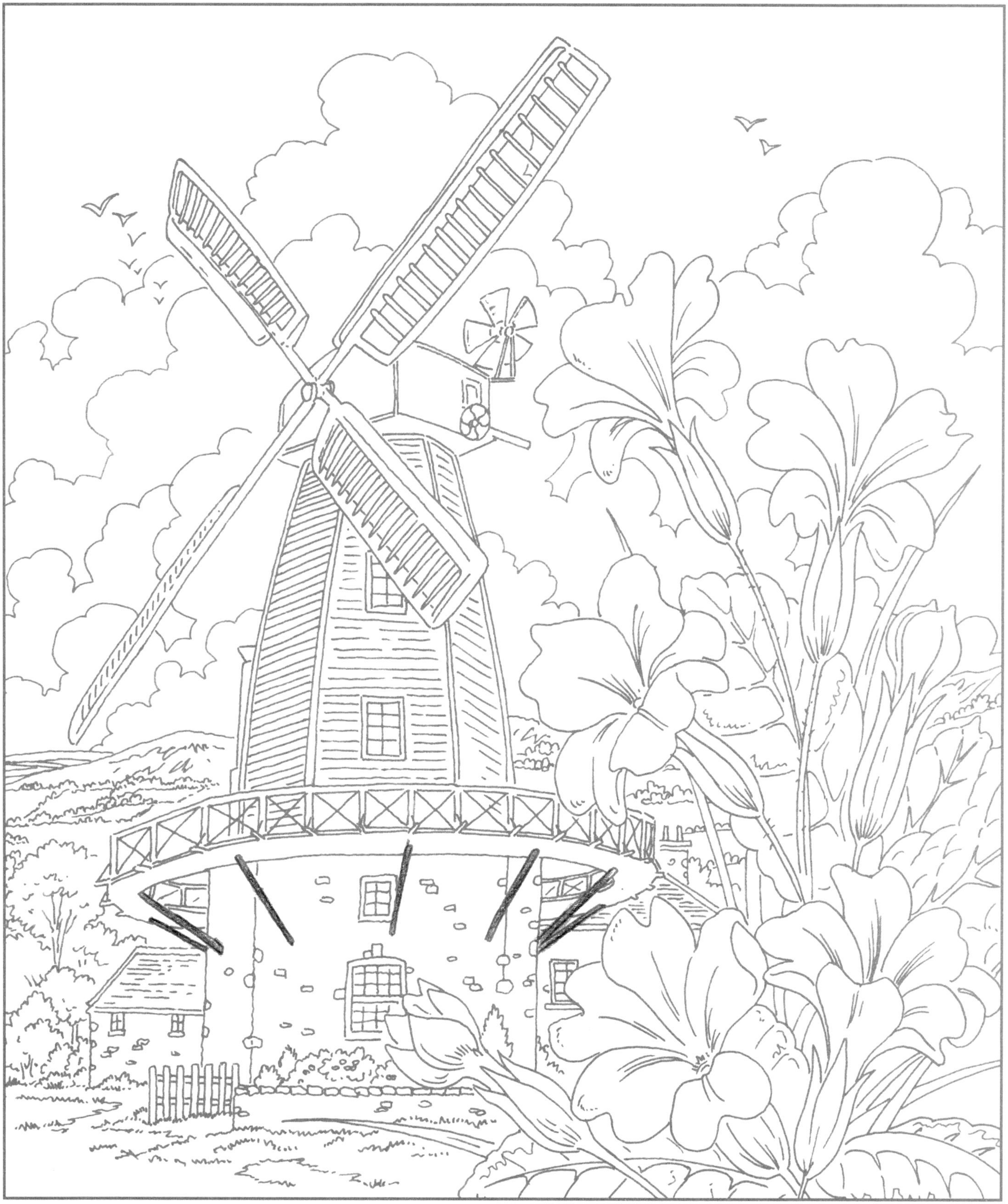

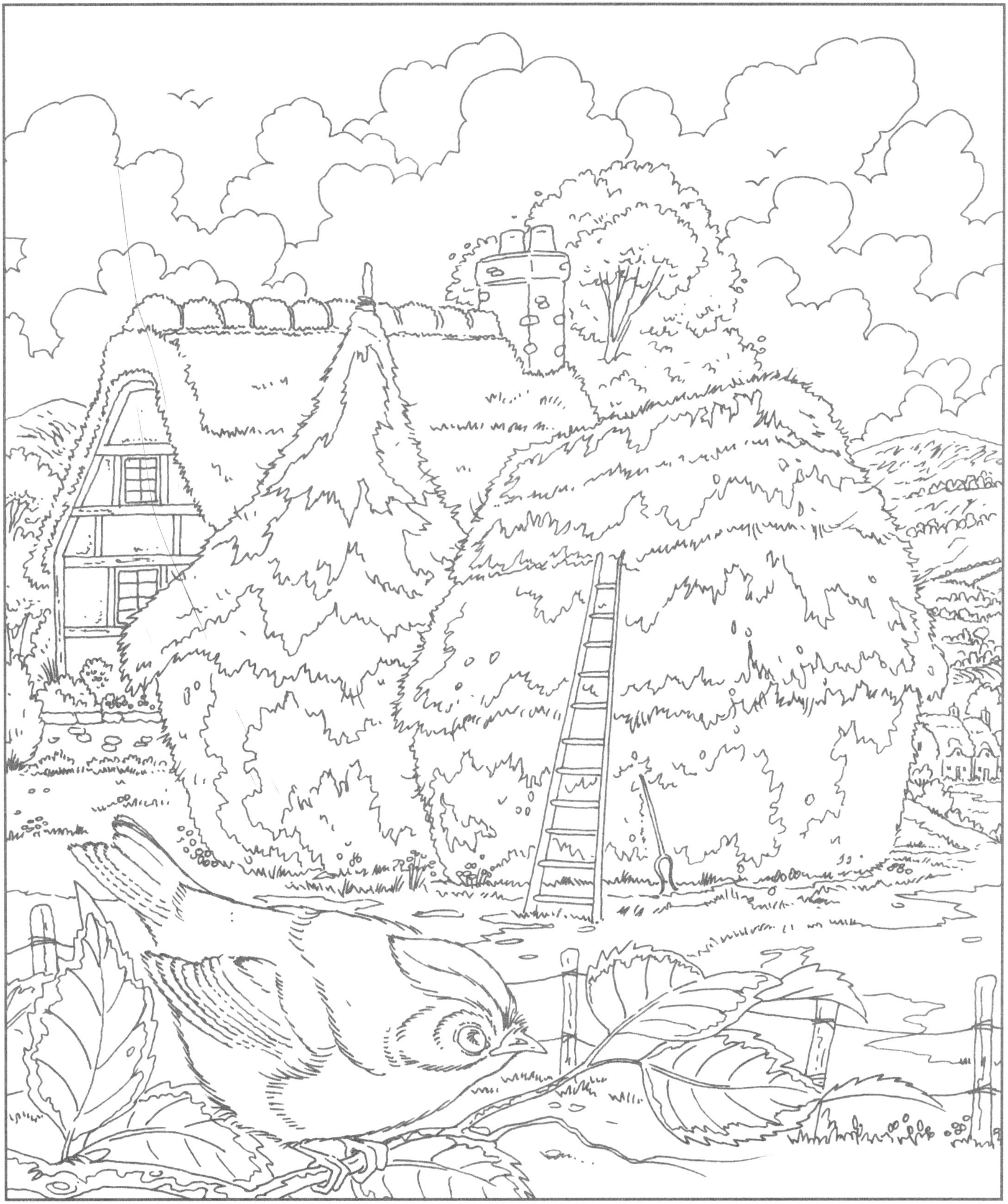

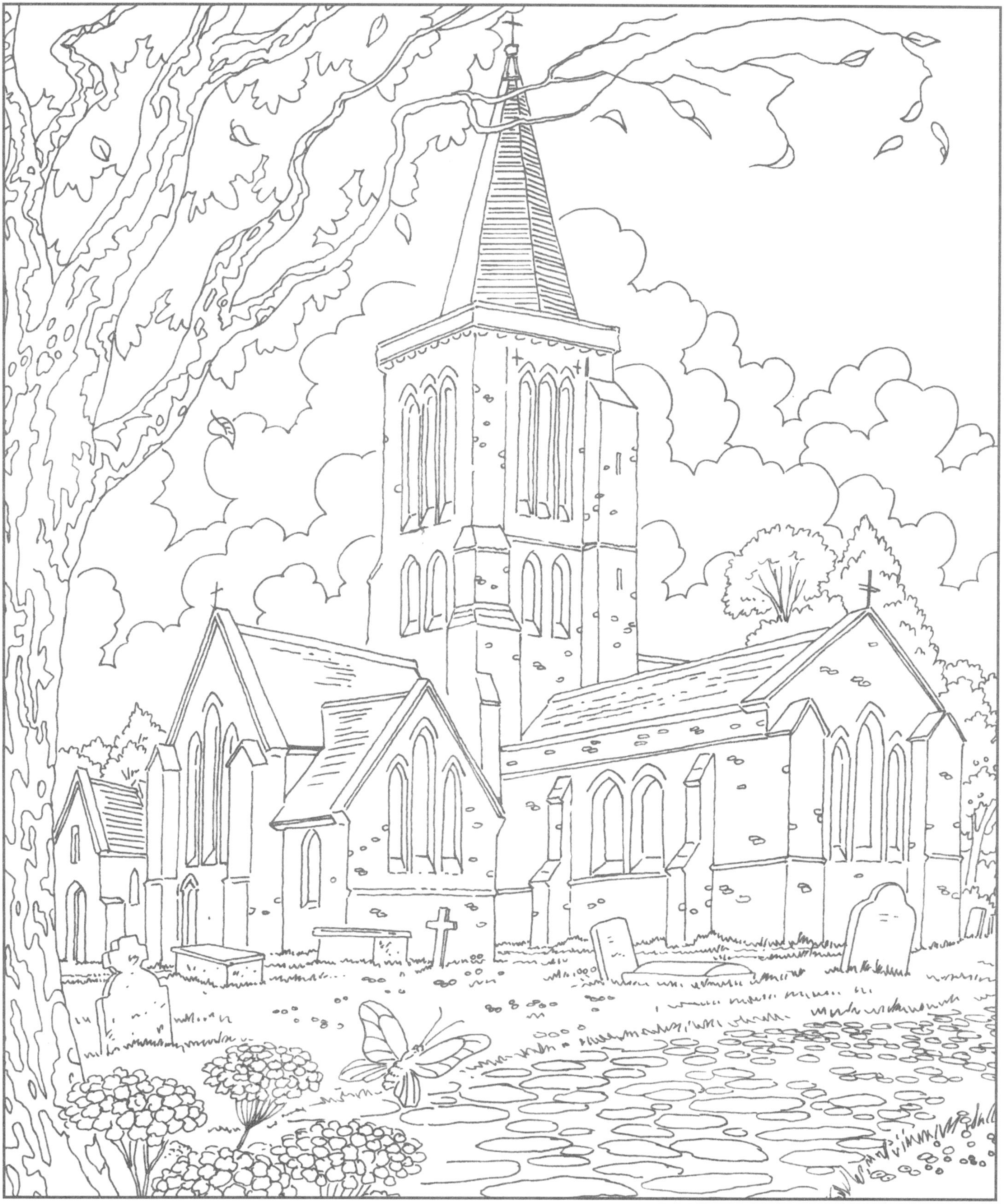

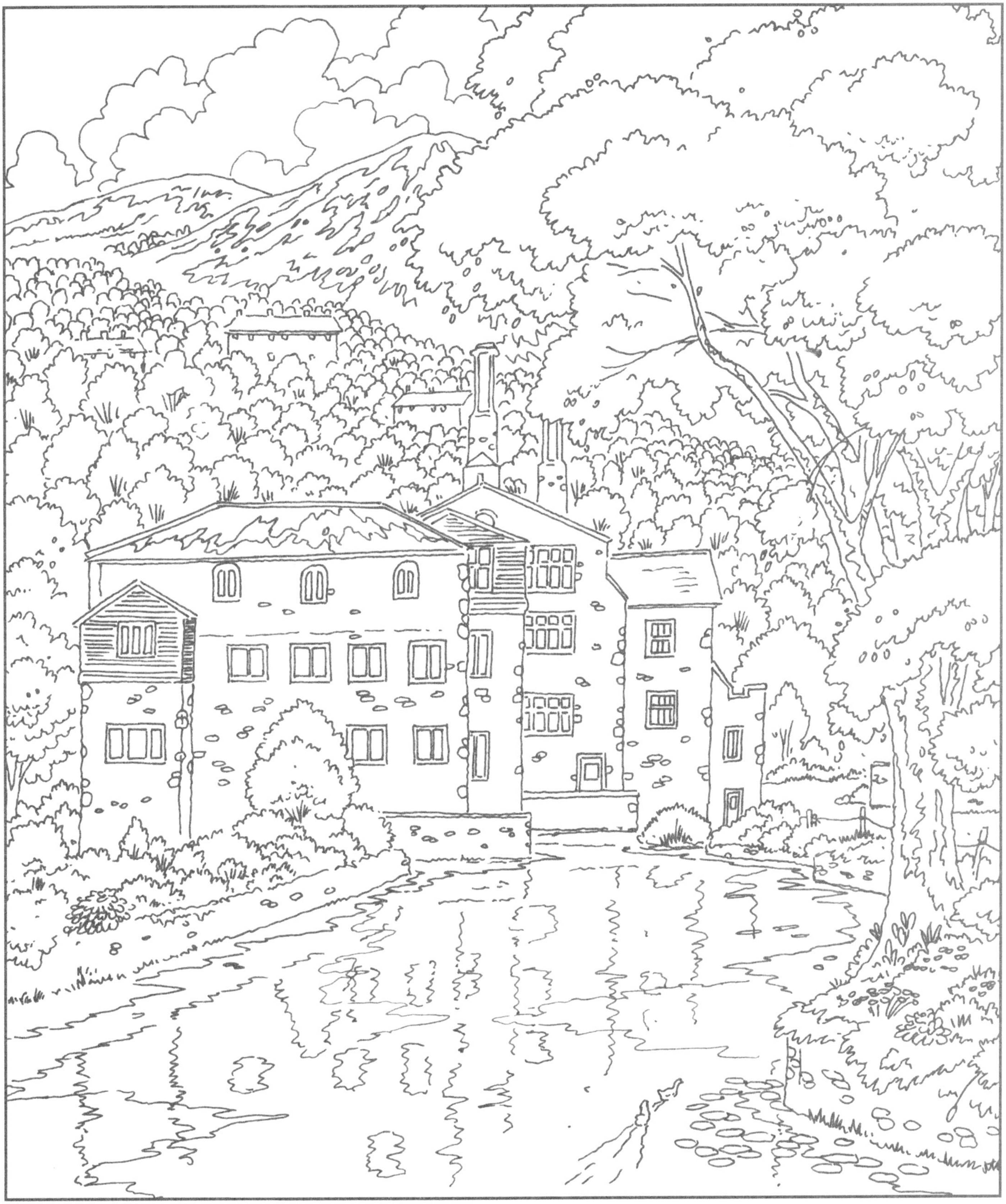

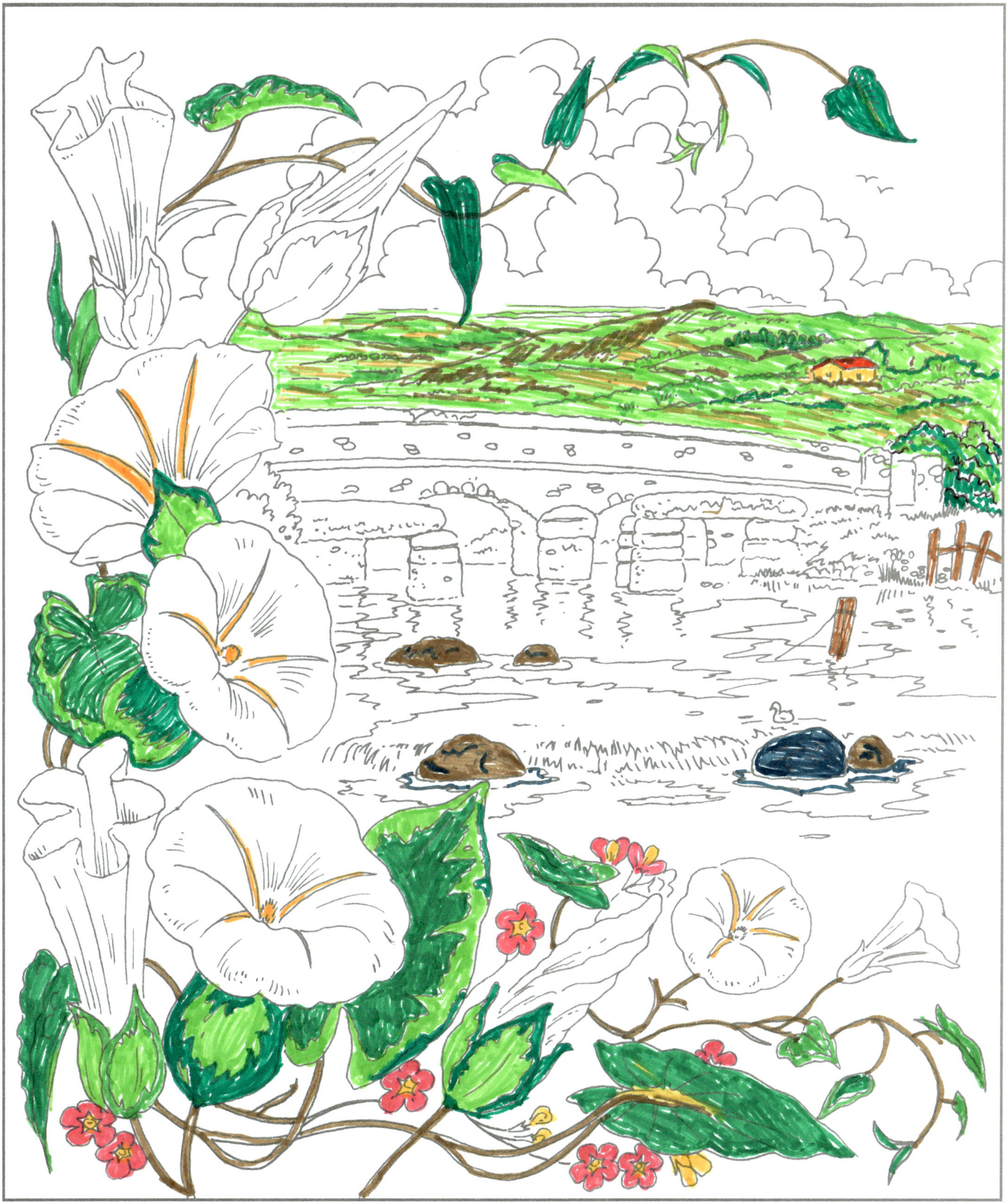

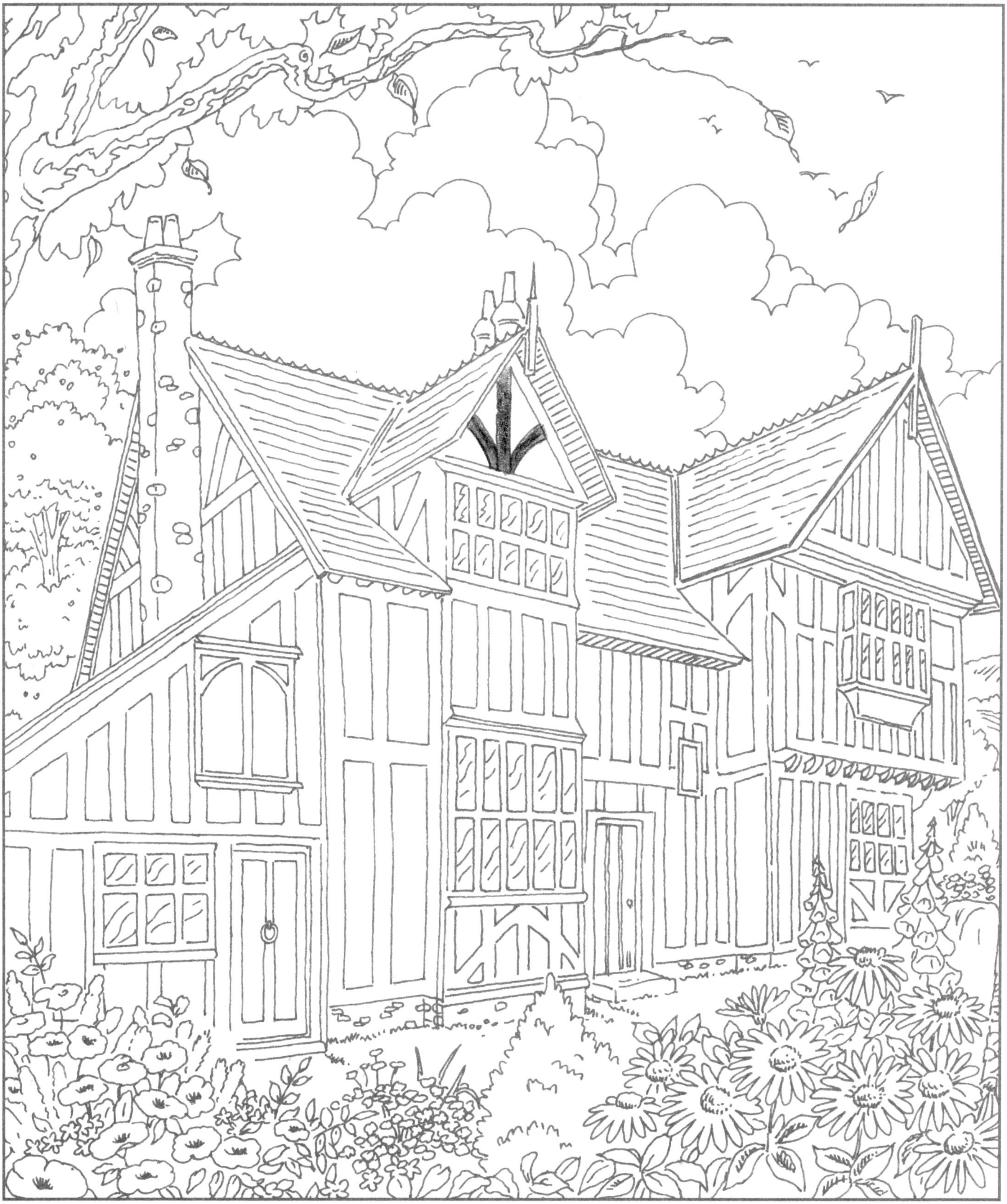

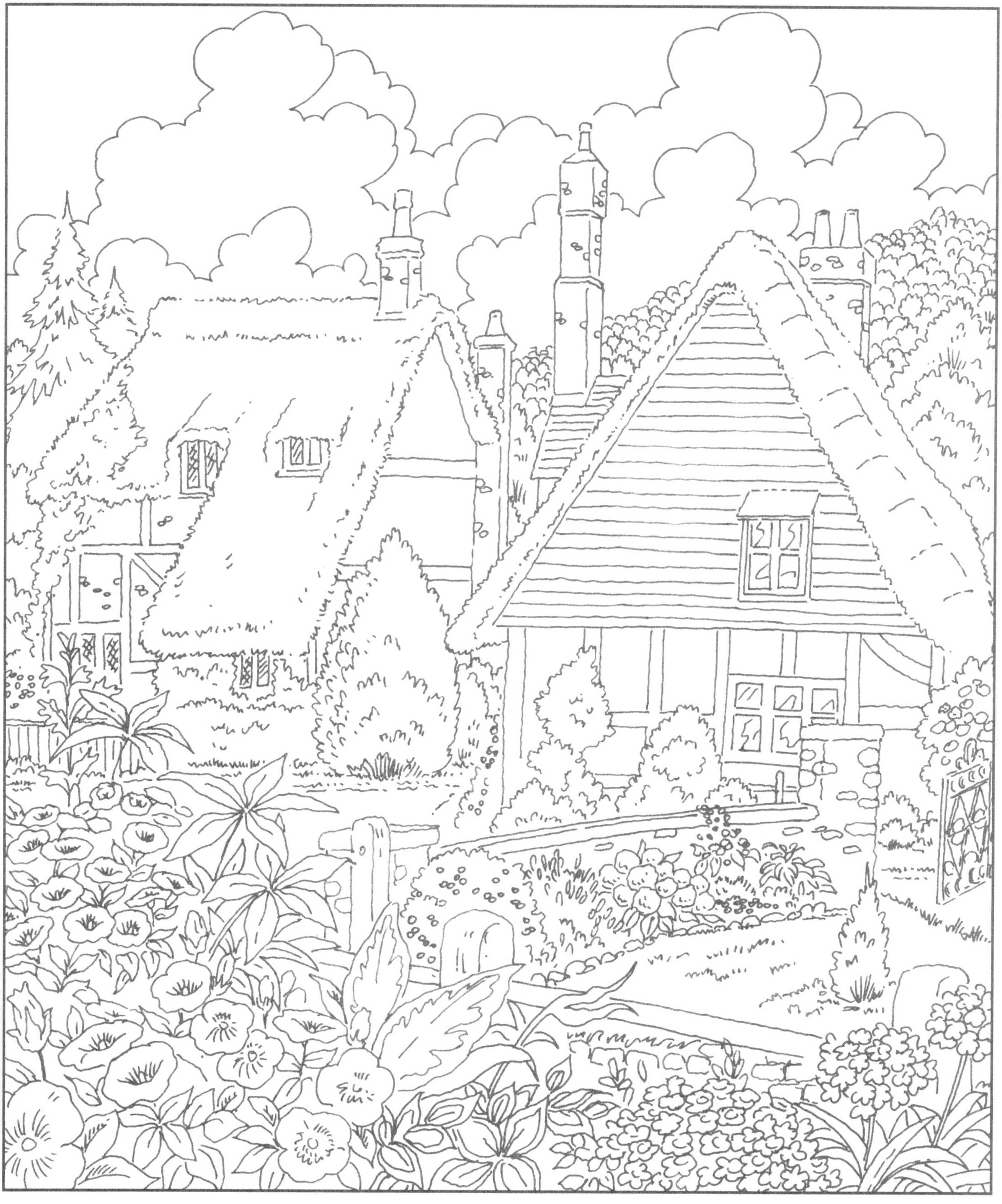

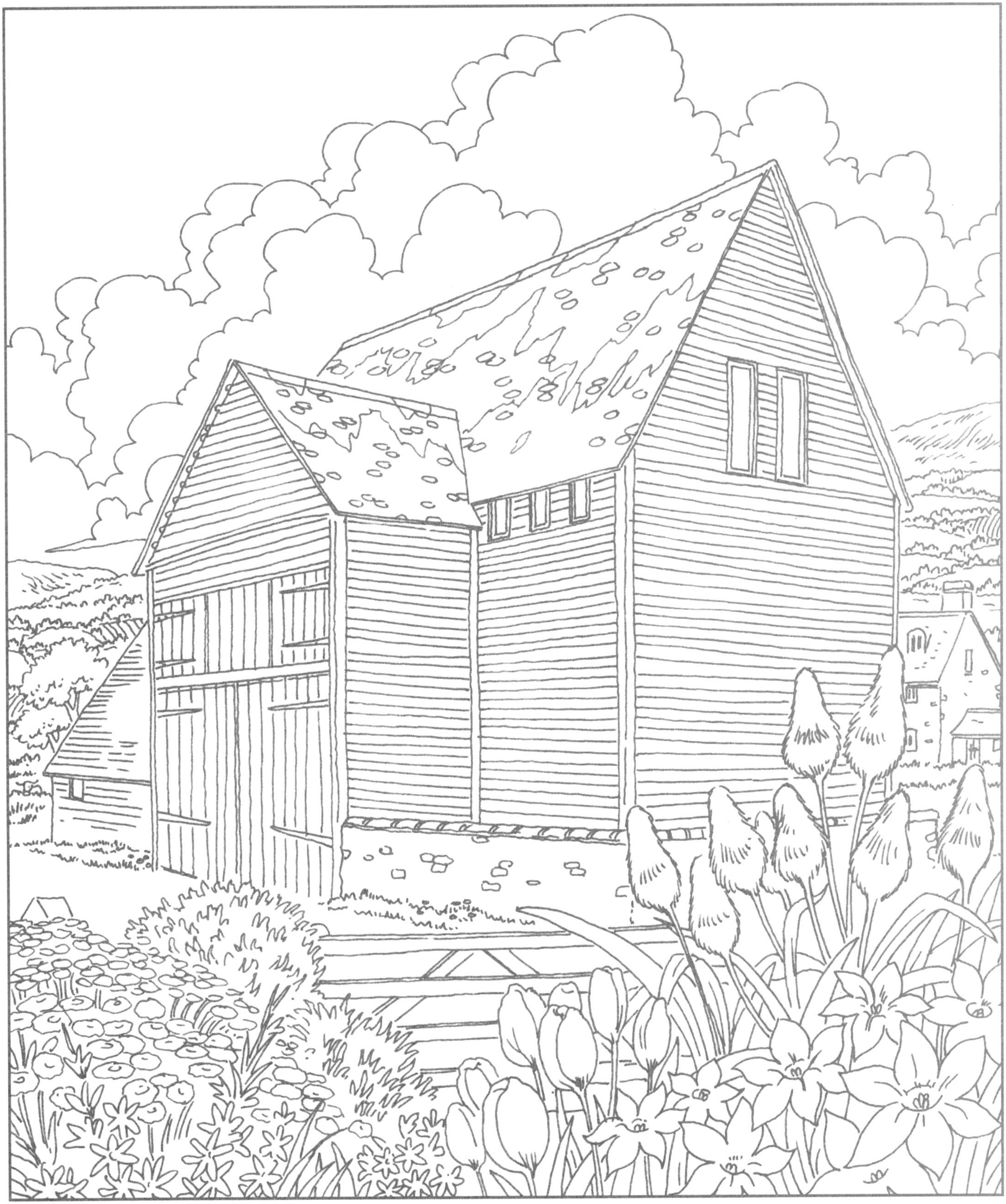

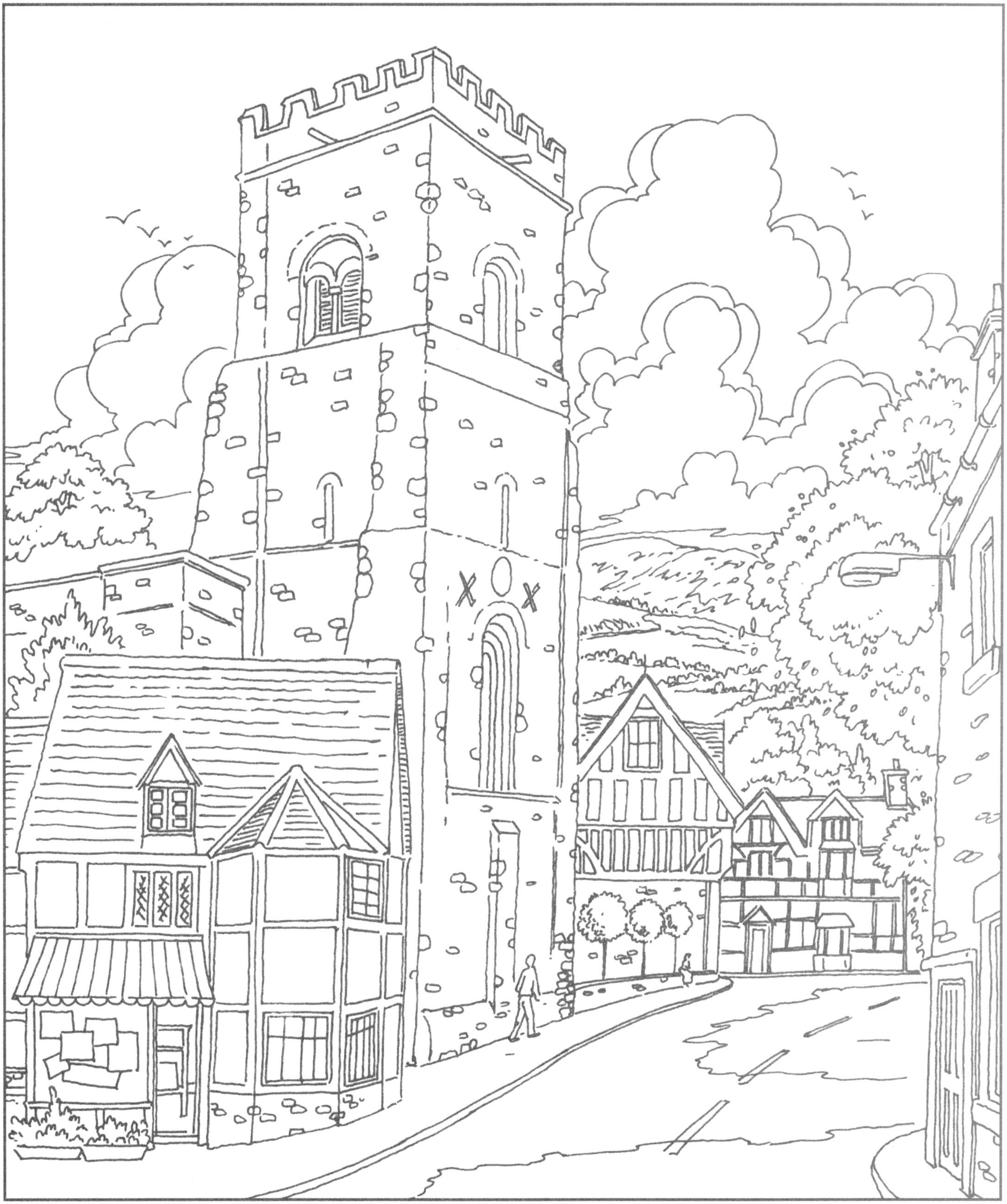

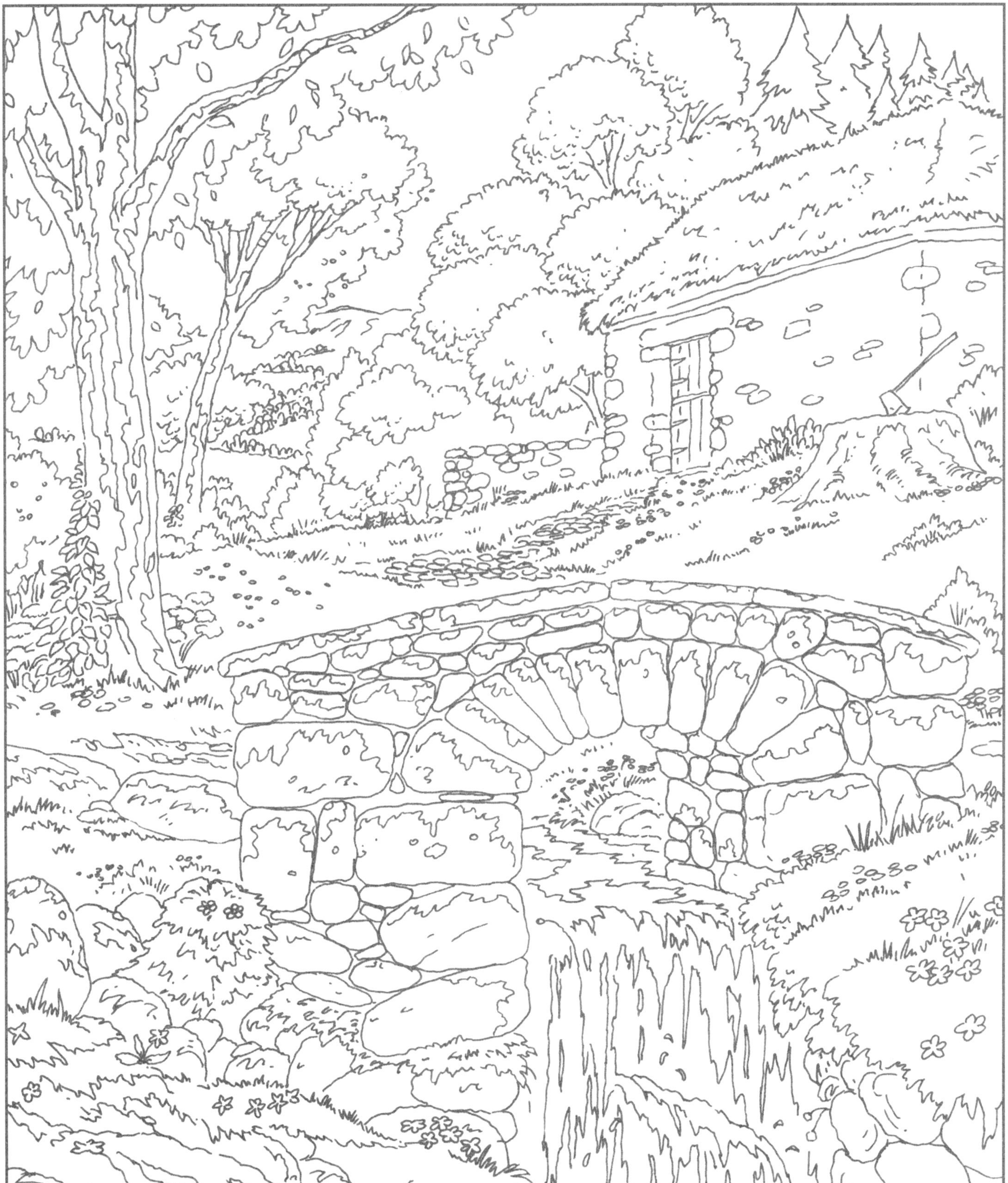

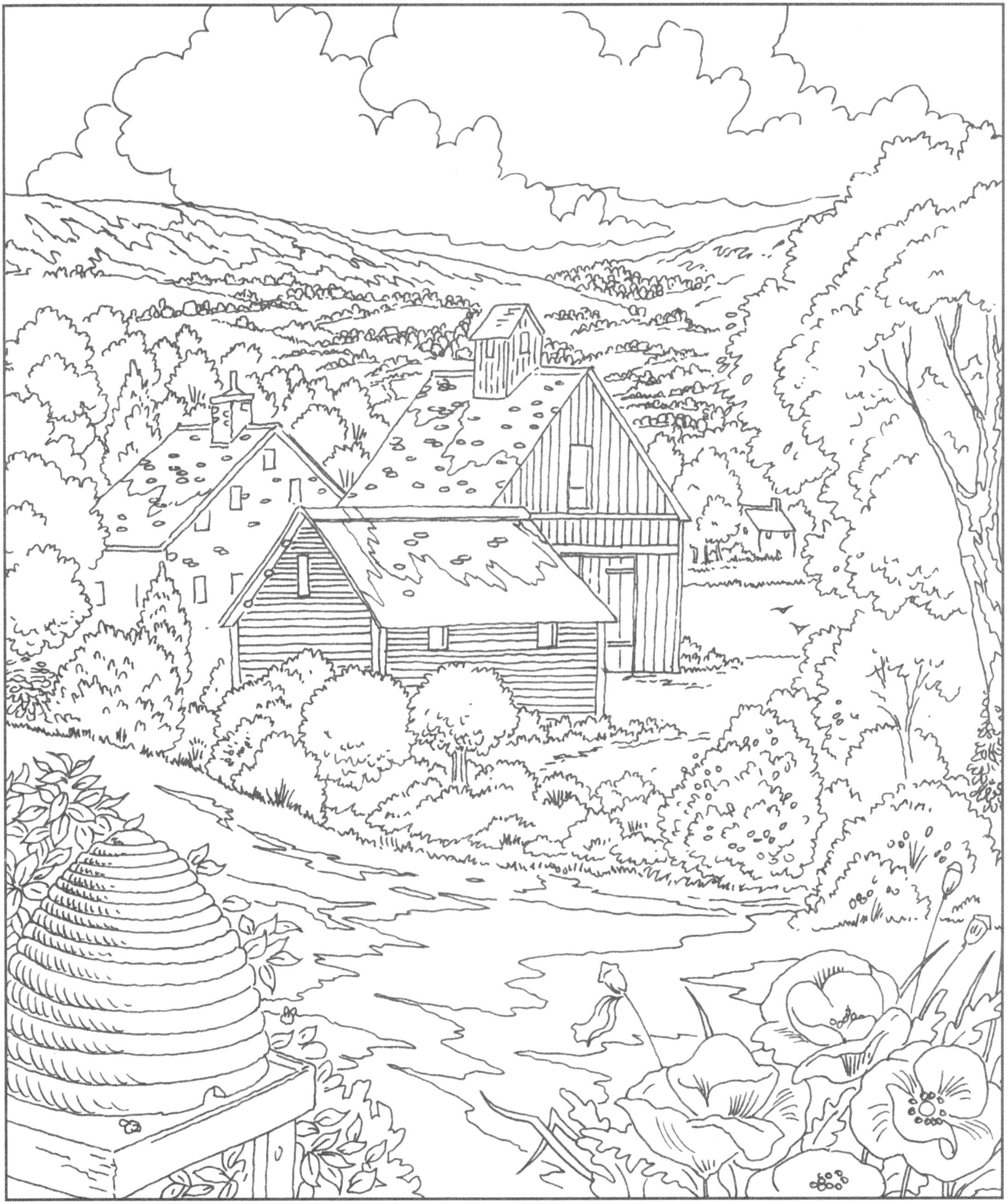

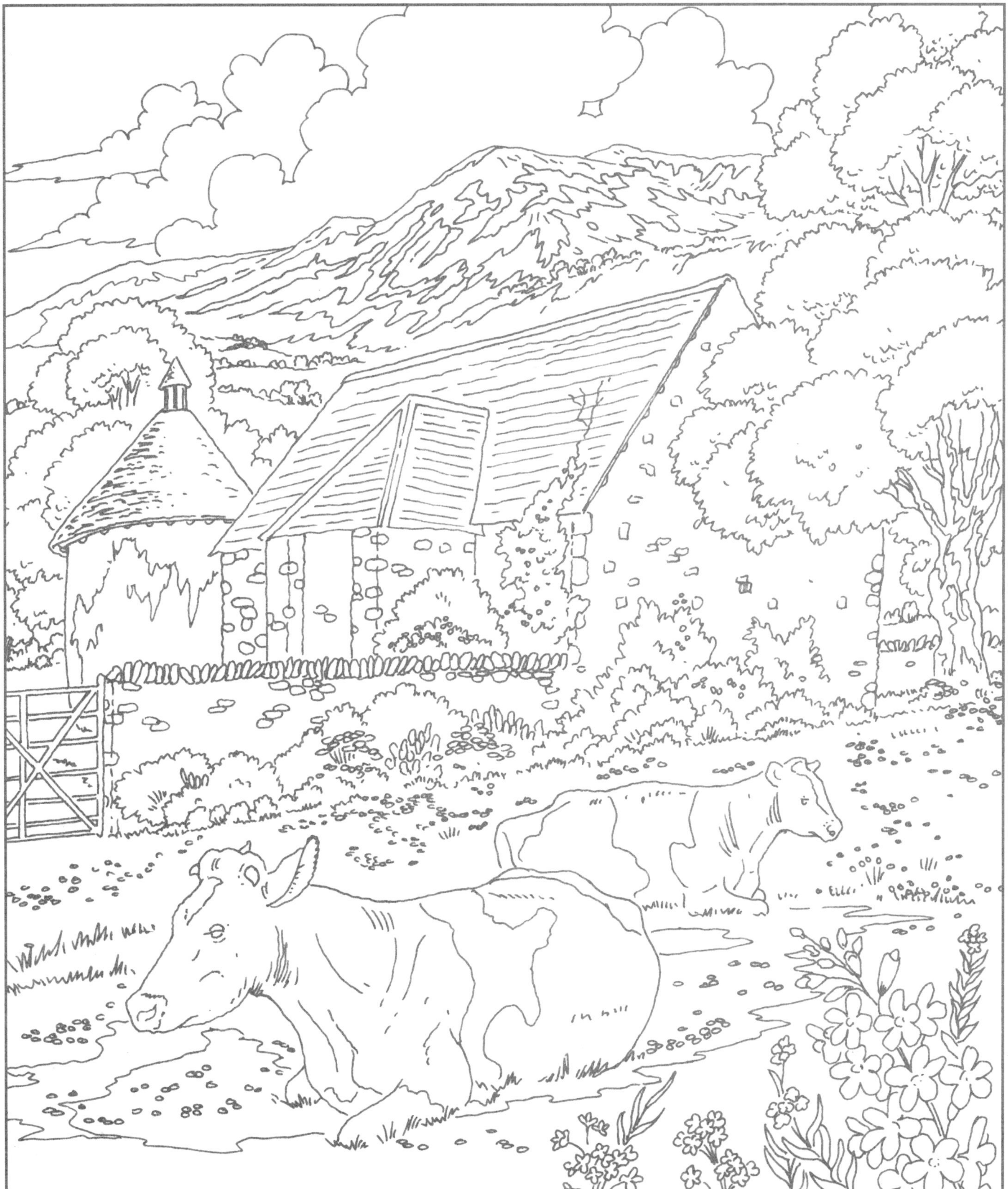

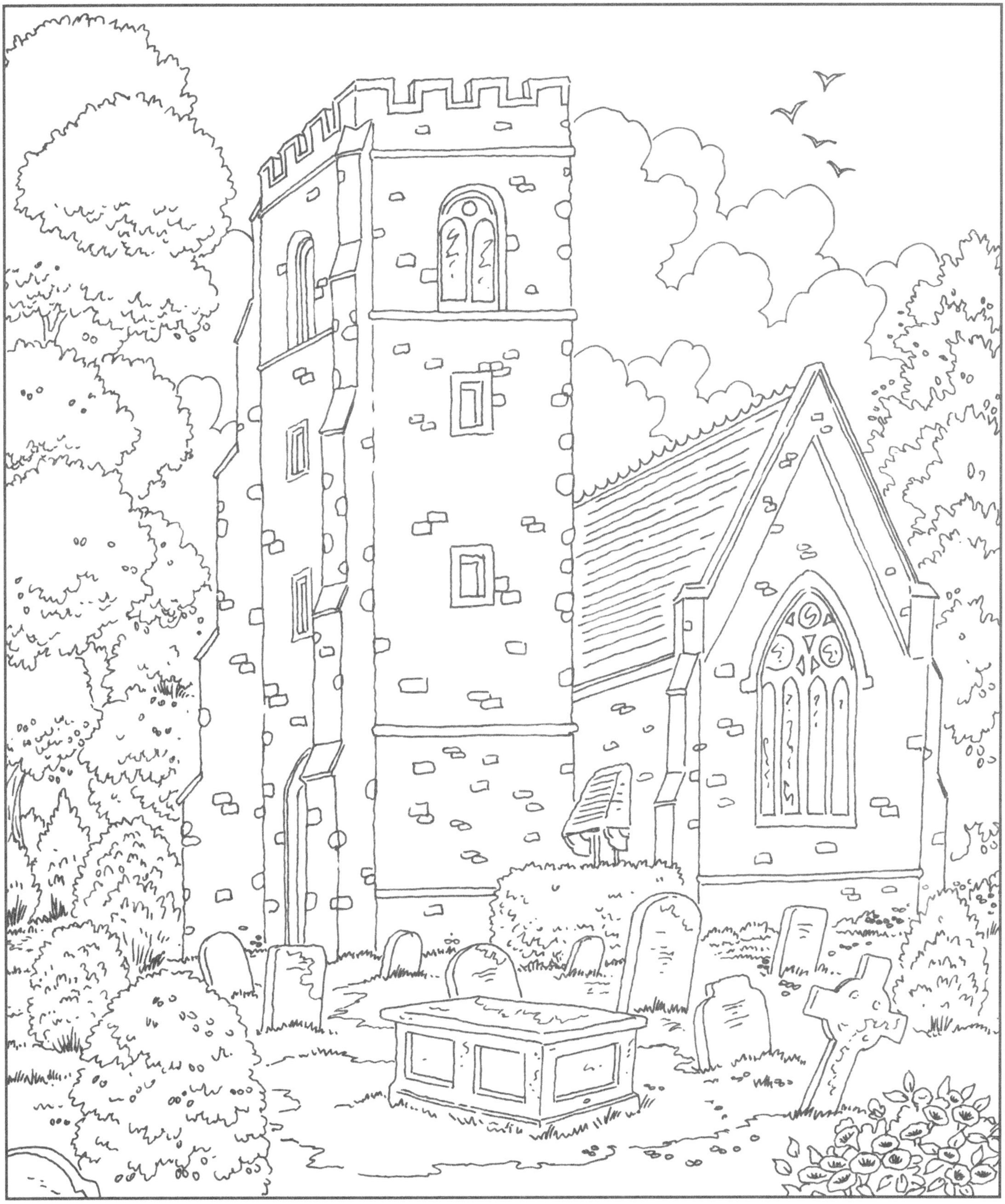

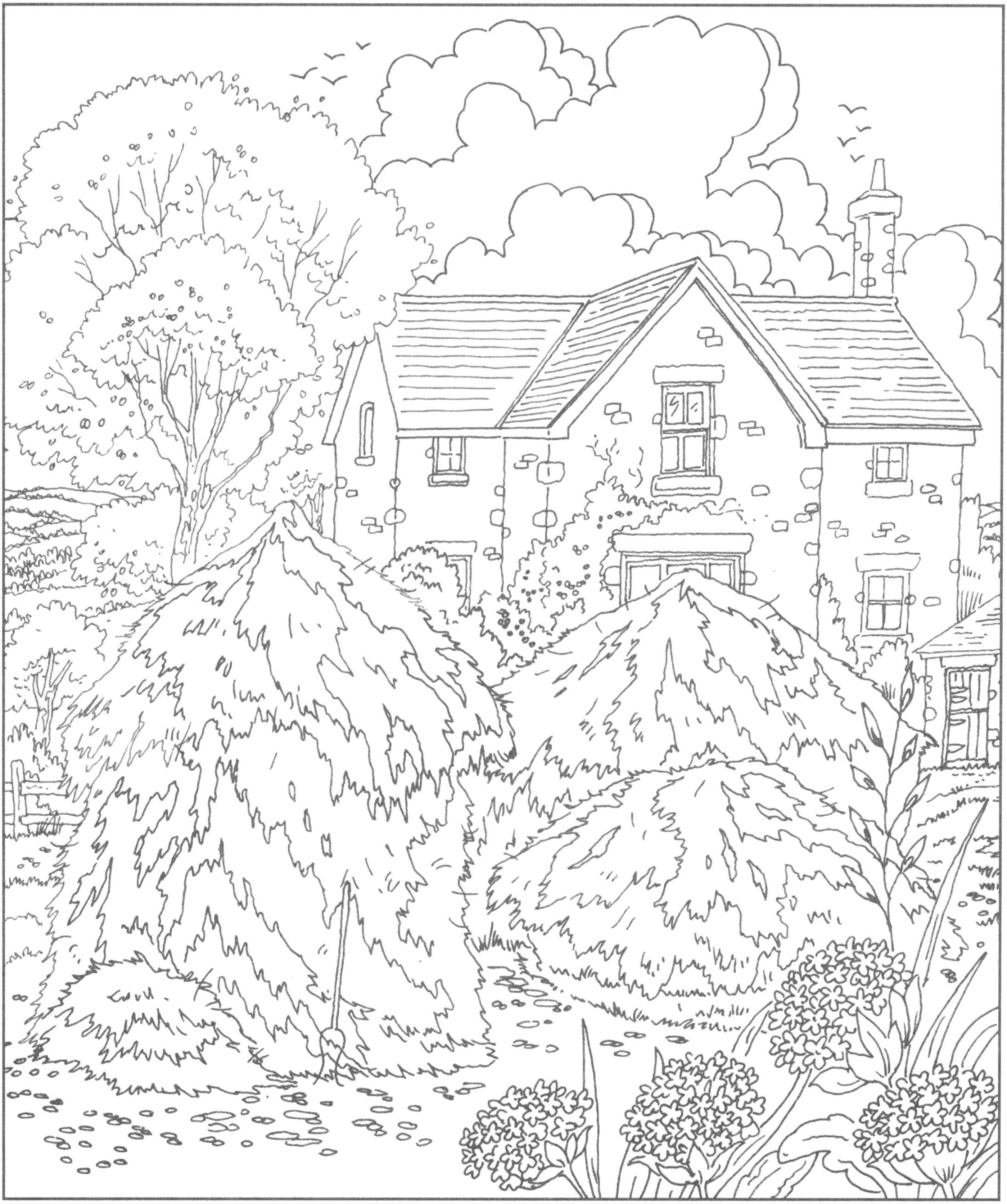

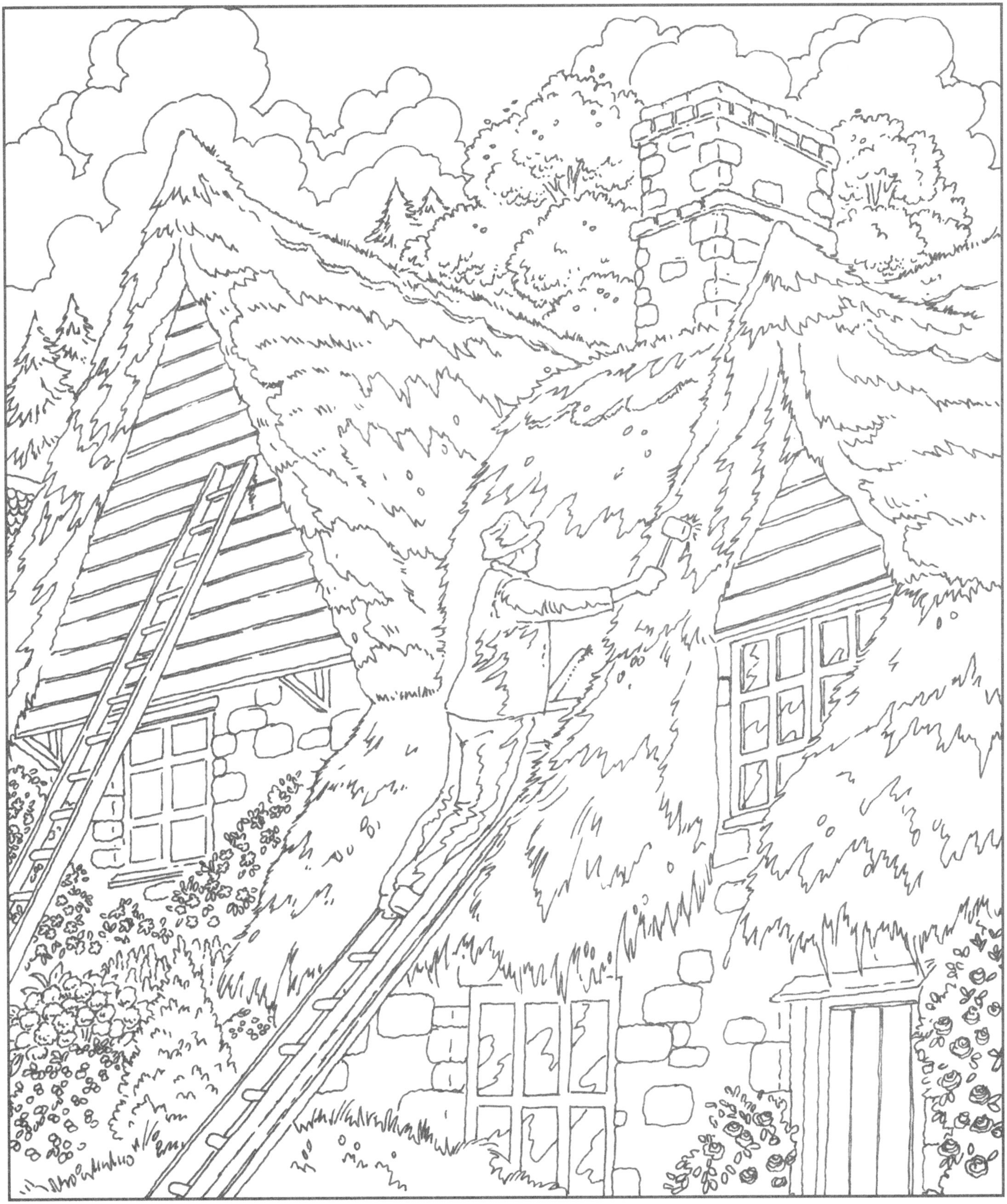

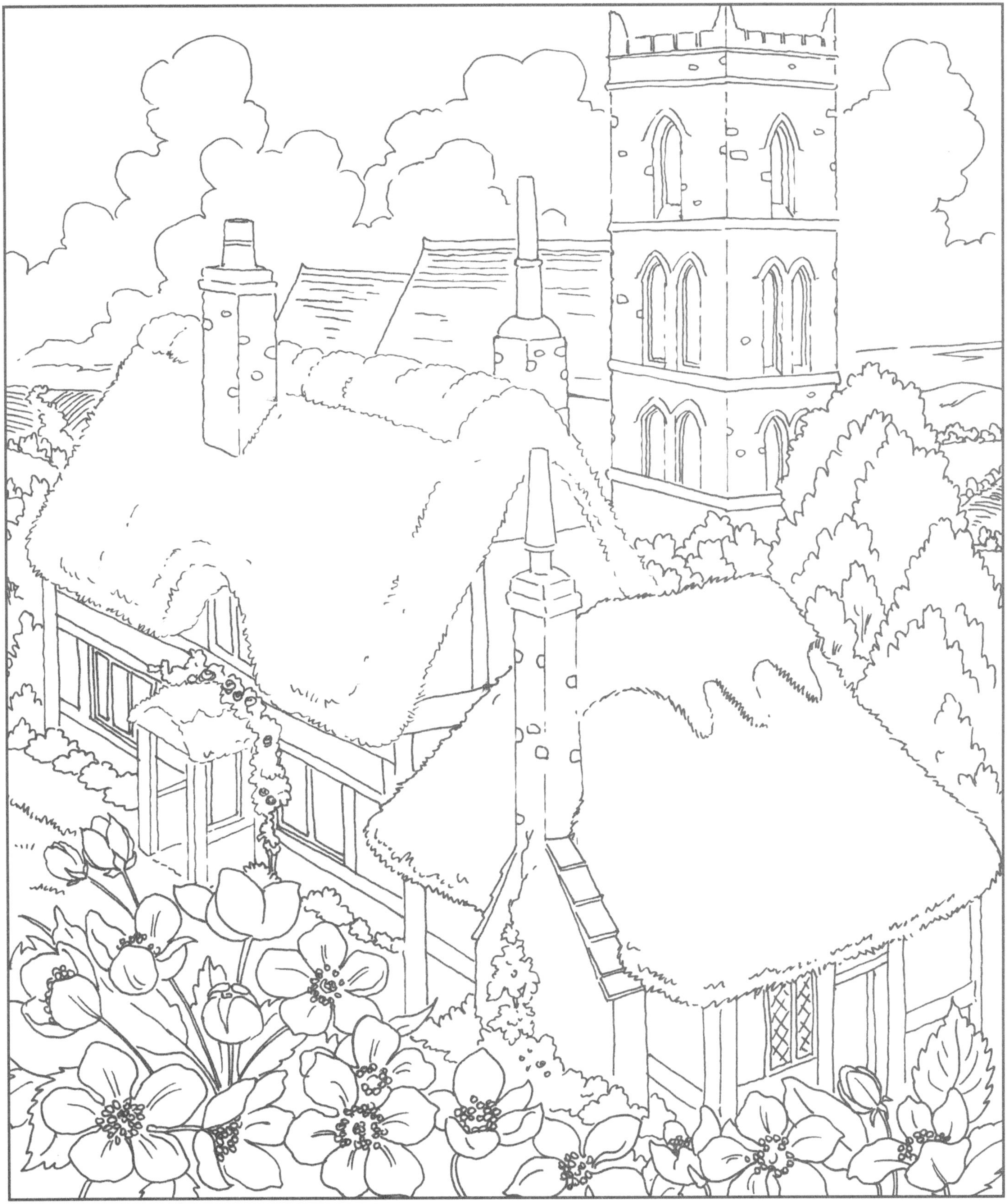

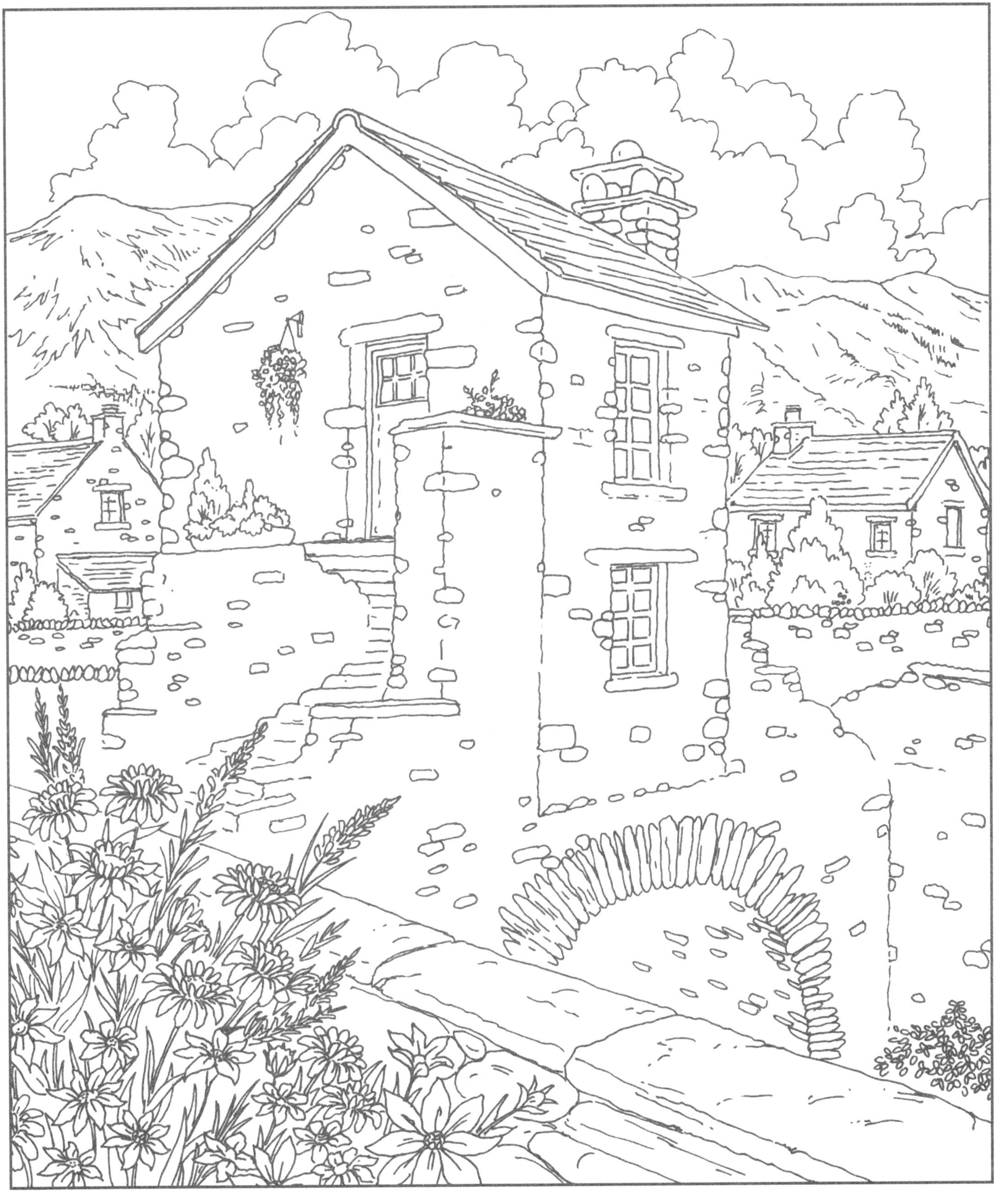

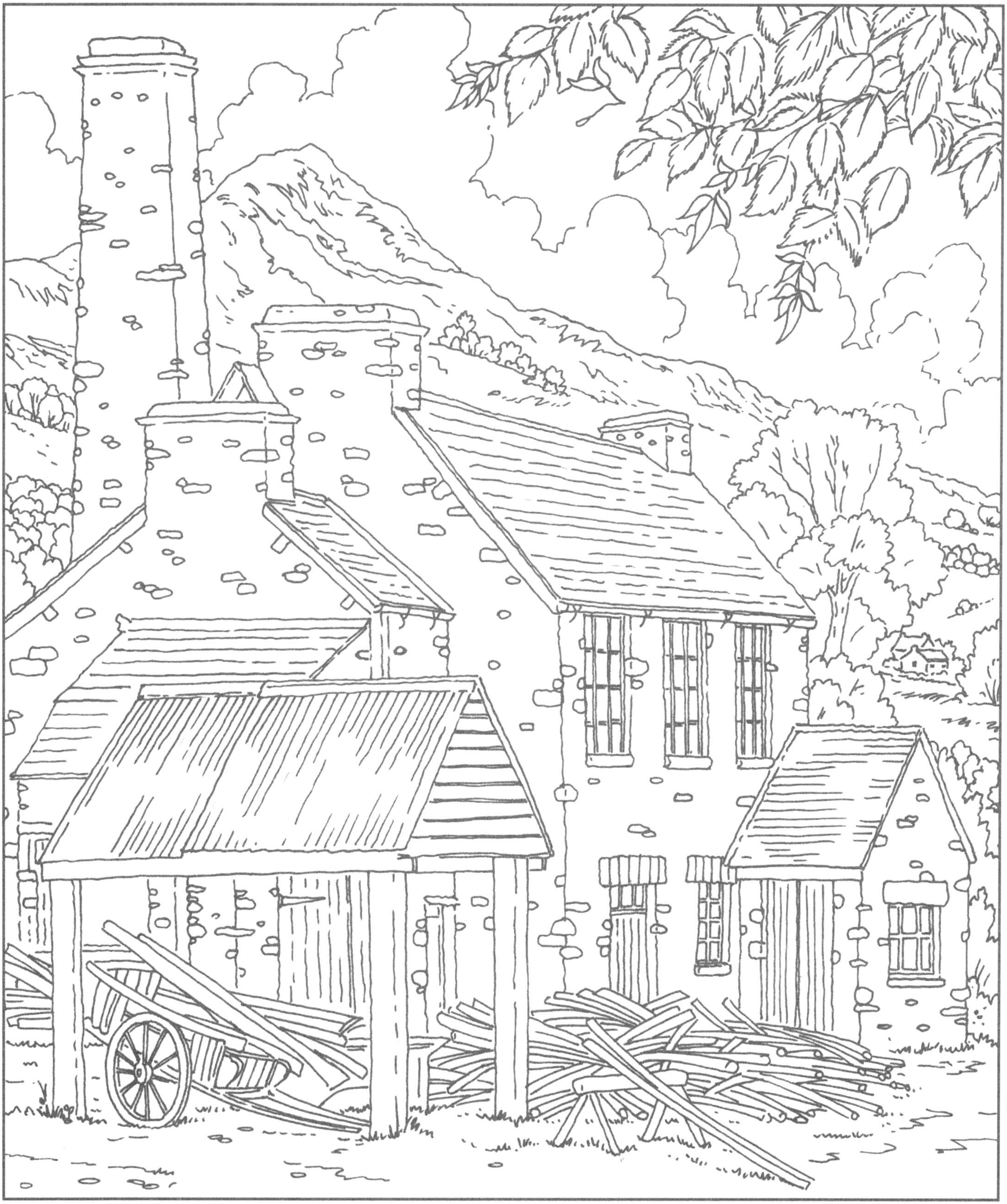

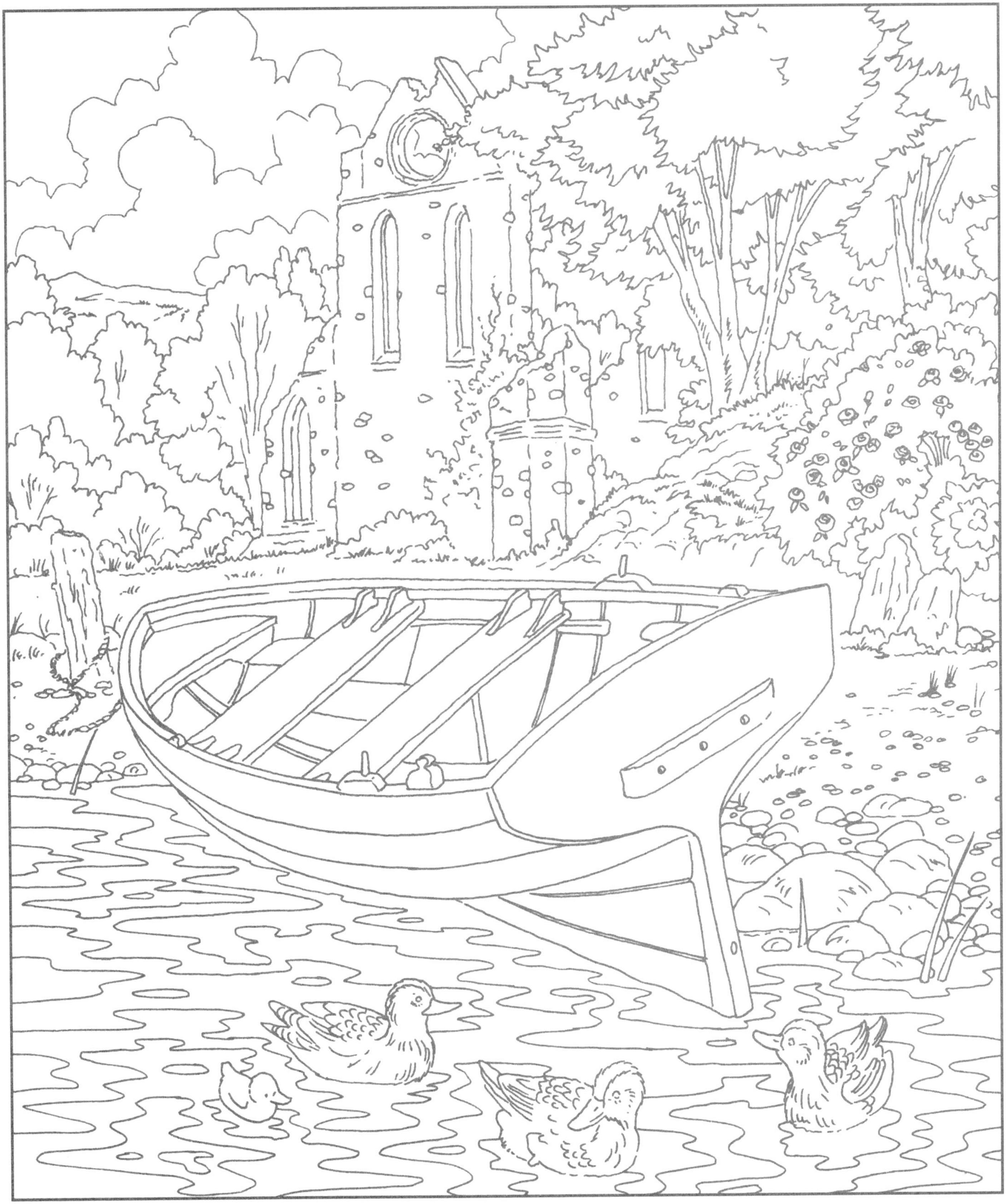

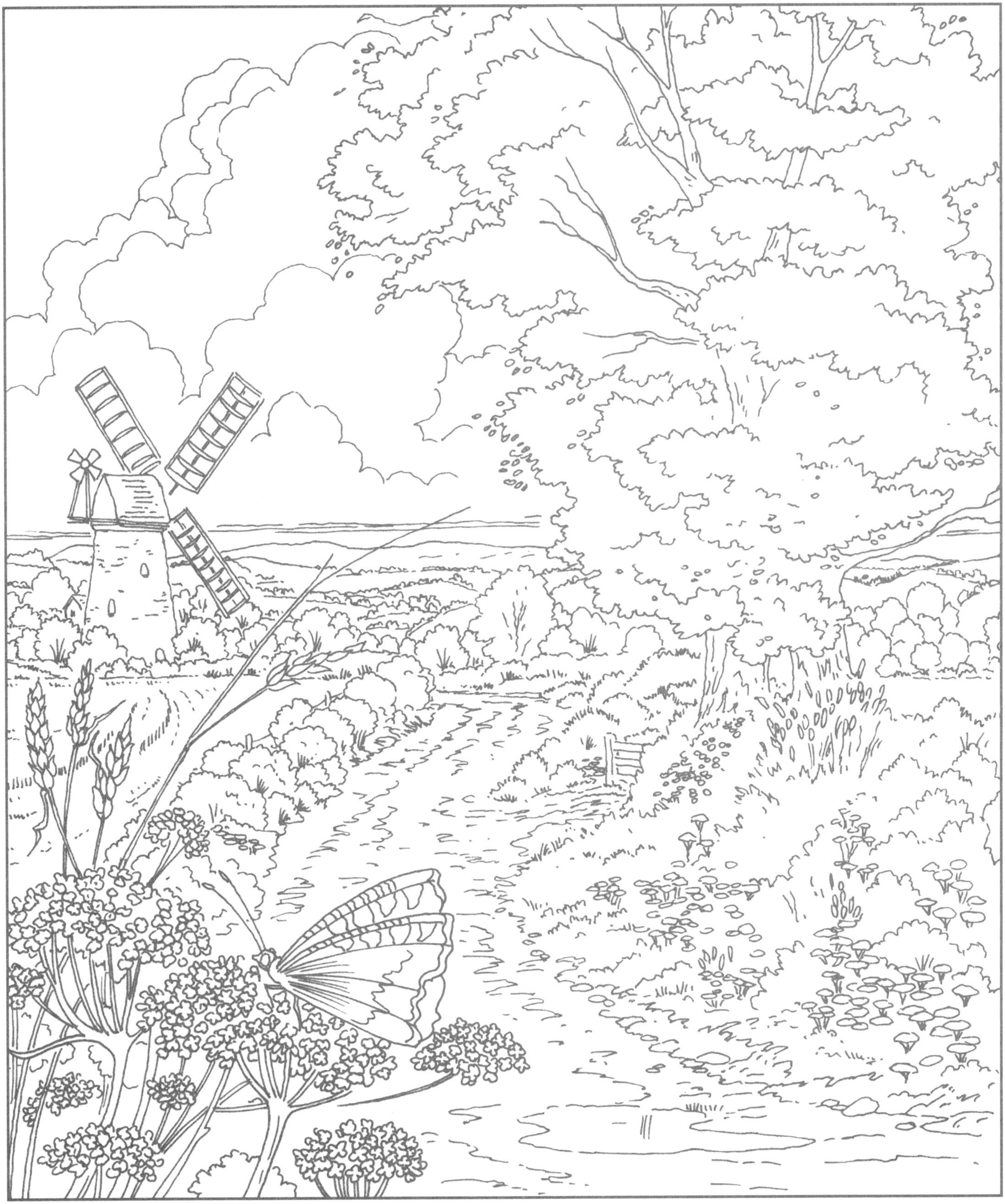

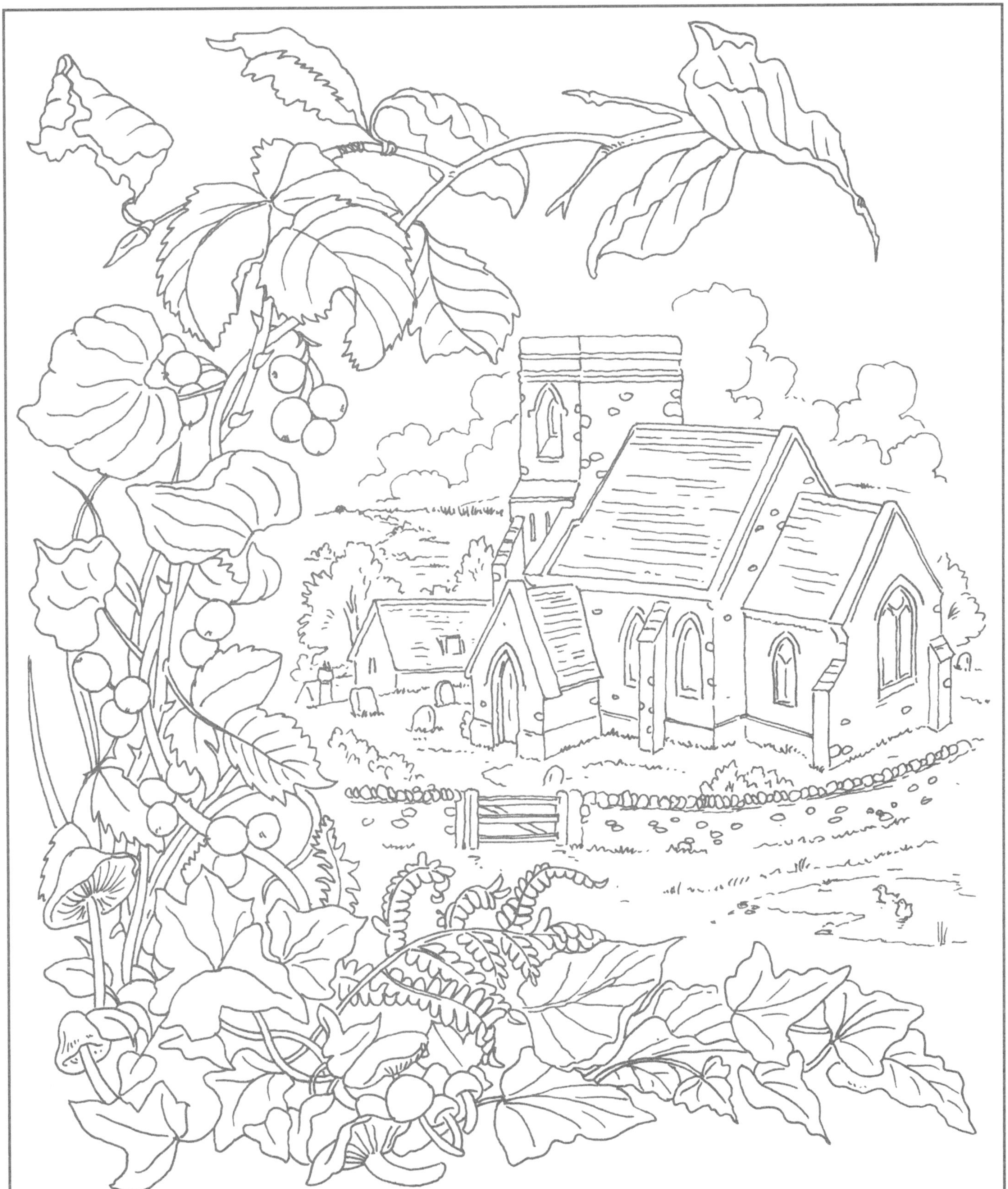

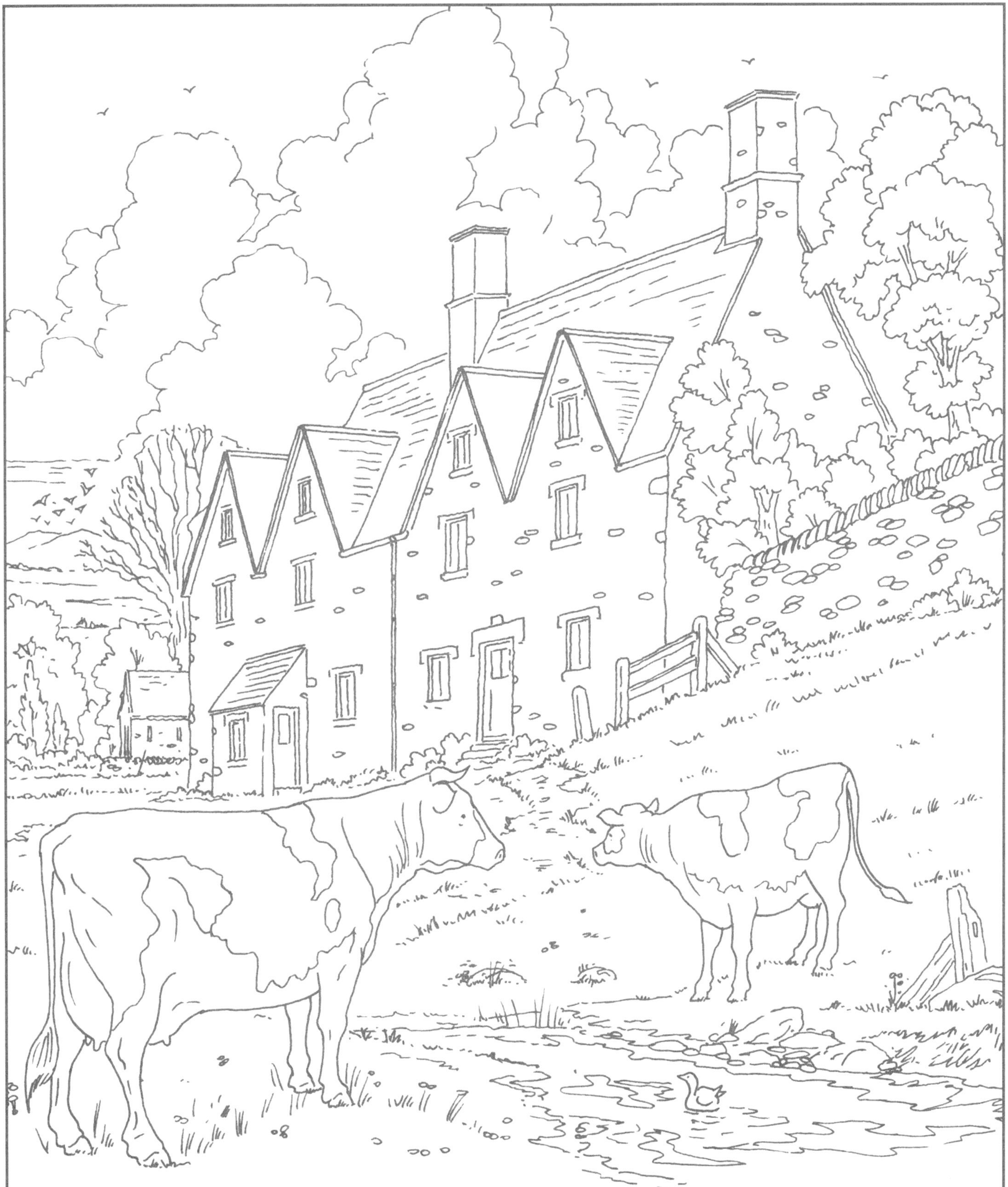

Six Weeks At The War...

Millicent Sutherland (Duchess of)

Nabu Public Domain Reprints:

You are holding a reproduction of an original work published before 1923 that is in the public domain in the United States of America, and possibly other countries. You may freely copy and distribute this work as no entity (individual or corporate) has a copyright on the body of the work. This book may contain prior copyright references, and library stamps (as most of these works were scanned from library copies). These have been scanned and retained as part of the historical artifact.

This book may have occasional imperfections such as missing or blurred pages, poor pictures, errant marks, etc. that were either part of the original artifact, or were introduced by the scanning process. We believe this work is culturally important, and despite the imperfections, have elected to bring it back into print as part of our continuing commitment to the preservation of printed works worldwide. We appreciate your understanding of the imperfections in the preservation process, and hope you enjoy this valuable book.

The "Millicent Sutherland Ambulance" at the Hague.

SIX WEEKS AT THE WAR

BY
Millicent, Duchess of Sutherland

CHICAGO
A. C. McCLURG & CO.
1915

Albert A. Sprague

To
LES SŒURS DE NOTRE DAME DE NAMUR,
who sheltered us.

To
Dr. OSWALD MORGAN, of Guy's Hospital, and Sisters BARTLETT, HERON-WATSON, VIZARD, FORD, KIRBY, COWELL, NETHERWOOD, THAKE, and Mr. C. WINSER, stretcher bearer, of the "Millicent Sutherland Ambulance," on whose courage, confidence, and skill I relied so much, I dedicate this book.

Allons, courons porter nos pas
 Dans tous les lieux où l'on respire ;
Affrontons glaces et verglas,
  Louons ce Dieu qui nous inspire !

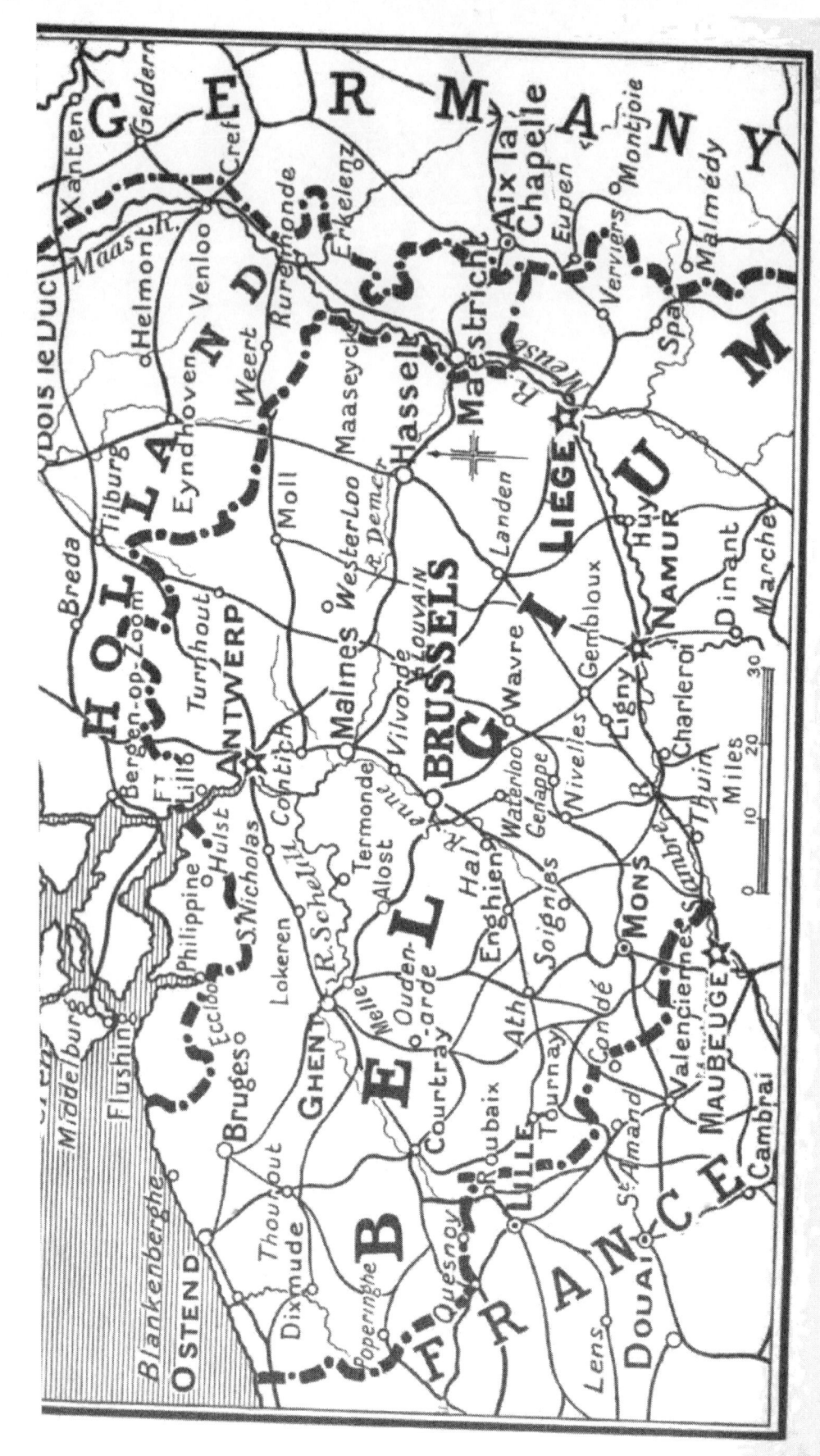

Map of Belgium.

CONTENTS.

CHAPTER		PAGE
I.	OFF TO THE WAR	1
II.	IN WAR-SWEPT BELGIUM	10
III.	DAYS AND NIGHTS OF HORROR AT NAMUR	26
IV.	LIFE AMONG THE INVADERS	44
V.	THROUGH THE GERMAN LINES IN A MILITARY TRAIN	56
VI.	THE HIDEOUS HAVOC OF WAR	75
VII.	OUT OF GERMANY'S CLUTCHES	82

LIST OF ILLUSTRATIONS.

PLATE		FACES PAGE
I.	THE "MILLICENT SUTHERLAND AMBULANCE" AT THE HAGUE	*Frontispiece.*
II.	MAP OF BELGIUM	vii.
III.	SOME OF OUR WOUNDED, BELGIAN AND FRENCH	7
IV.	GERMAN SOLDIERS GUARDING THE BURNING OF THE MARKET PLACE	23
V.	A CORNER OF NAMUR AFTER THE FIRE	39
VI.	OUR GERMAN GUARDS OUTSIDE THE CONVENT	55
VII.	ENGLISH SOLDIERS IN A BELGIAN MANSION AT HARVENGT NOT FAR FROM MONS, UNDER THE CARE OF COUNT MAXINE DE BOUSIES—IRISH GUARDS, IRISH RIFLES, ROYAL SCOTS, ETC.	71
VIII.	ON THE ROAD TO MAUBEUGE	87
IX.	HOUSE DESTROYED BY SHELL ON ROUTE TO MAUBEUGE	95
X.	OUR AMBULANCE AT NAMUR	103
XI.	THE PASS OF THE COMMANDANT OF NAMUR TO ENABLE THE DUCHESS TO GO TO MAUBEUGE	110
XII.	THE PASS OF THE GOVERNOR OF MAUBEUGE ALLOWING THE DUCHESS TO RETURN TO ENGLAND	111

INTRODUCTION.

It is difficult to write an introduction to one's own book, and especially to a few rough diary notes strung together in a hurry to meet the exigencies of the hour.

I have been asked to convey an impression of the German invasion of Belgium during the first weeks of the war.

But it must be remembered that I had no opportunity of judging passing events as a whole. In every place the Germans occupied they immediately built an impregnable wall of restrictions and spread false news to exclude true information.

These restrictions exercised a complete censorship over outside movements. I could only study the German, firstly, by his attitude towards our Ambulance, secondly, by his attitude towards the population of the town in which I found myself, and, thirdly, by the attitude of the German private soldiers with whom I came in contact.

Fighting Germany, suddenly forced on to one's horizon, is imposing. She sets out to be imposing. I noticed it was an essential part of her war tactics to achieve a "moral effect."

The theatrical display which was characteristic of the march of the German troops through Brussels, the scenic arrangement of all the paraphernalia of war, cavalry, infantry, formidable artillery, air craft, and every conceivable adjunct of transport and scientific military mechanism, attained this result.

In a lesser degree the same thing happened at Namur. Unfortunately Namur is not an open city so she suffered for a short time from horrors worse than "moral effect" —she suffered the cruelty that only a conqueror like the Prussian conceives.

To my nurses and doctor and to me the Germans showed civility. I do not attempt to probe for the motive. Germany has always been jealous of England, and during this fearful war she has grown to hate our country, but I am persuaded that her *respect* for England is unchanged. The Germans certainly showed respect to English women, so far as my Ambulance was concerned. I am glad that I could

INTRODUCTION.

speak their language and I am grateful for their appreciation of our work. Under military despotism one is grateful for any consideration.

This war is a ghastly psychological study. For long Prussia's rulers have prepared a machine which is scientifically so remarkable and in detail so formidable that the varying component parts of the German Army, which is now practically the German nation, have been forced into a blind belief in it. In this war Germany is trusting the Prussian machine without protest and becoming entangled in its actions and reactions. Yet by every law of progress, by every law of race emancipation, the German nation, through this belief, is deliberately destroying itself.

Germany was brutally harsh in Belgium, but she acted on a preconcerted plan. Her later atrocities and unworthy expediencies in this fearful struggle are merely the result of a suspicion of her own approaching failure. If there is failure in one part or another of Germany's iron machine, barbarities will be summoned to the aid of strategy. This is only to be expected. The millions of soldiers at war must not be so sternly blamed as the machine that drives them; they have been so long bewildered by it, so long have given their souls into its keeping.

I think a German will never admit failure until he has had to bite the dust. Bernhardi declares that for Germany no half measures are possible—World Conquest or Downfall. Only people with little imagination and without a sense of humour can believe so uncritically in themselves, can so desperately challenge fate.

When Prussian military despotism is "Kaputt"—to use the Germans' favourite word about their foe, meaning "done"—the sense of security can return to the hearts of nations.

At tremendous sacrifice and through terrible experience, weak often by reason of our own shortcomings, troubled now and then by the things that might have been done and have been left undone, we are fighting to win in this war.

Not for our own hand alone shall we win, nor for the hands of our Allies. We fight for the liberties of the whole world.

And as we shall all gain Germany will also gain a nobler faith, a new spirit. She mothers a strong race and what is great in her history and in her character will be left her. Now she cannot even "see darkly." She is obsessed by her own false persuasions; her worthiest children are silent, and dare not speak; sooner or later she will acknowledge the truth, and if in that acknowledgment lies temporary humiliation, in it lies also Germany's deliverance.

MILLICENT SUTHERLAND.

CHAPTER I.

OFF TO THE WAR.

I LEFT England on August 8 to join the branch of the French Red Cross called "Secours Aux Blessés." The President is the Comtesse d'Haussonville. We steamed into Boulogne Harbour to the loud cheering of the crowds on the quay and cries of "Vive l'Angleterre." A Red Cross badge on that day seemed like a Legion of Honour, and from every mouth came the low murmur, "La Croix Rouge, La Croix Rouge ! C'est une Anglaise ! Ah ça, c'est bien ! " A little private, just recalled after five years' fighting in Morocco, insisted on carrying my rugs ; another man, "who would have been married to-morrow but for the war," my bag. I had no difficulty in getting through with my passports and French "laissez passer." An omnibus train was due to start in an hour from the Central Station. Everything was unusual, owing to the rapid mobilizing of the French Army.

I went to a restaurant and talked to the waiter over a ham sandwich and some red wine. He was a "réformé," and so debarred from military service.

What news did I know? he asked. He knew none. "Had the Germans taken Liége?" "Ces sacrés Allemands." My Red Cross seemed to carry an impression of general knowledge.

An old French lady rushed up to me and asked me if I knew what time the trains arrived at Lille, and "surely there would be no fighting there." An American inquired how long I had been in the profession. I began to see that I must assume an air of importance to cover my profound ignorance. When the engine drivers in Boulogne cheered me I felt fairly embarrassed.

I took my place amongst six for a slow night journey to Paris. They were interesting enough—my fellow passengers. A young French volunteer who had lived ten years in England began to talk about the awful 24 hours during which they thought England would not stand by France. This was refuted by Noël, the airman from Hendon, off to join the French Air Corps. A boy travelling through from Glasgow to Montauban was joining his regiment. A girl wished to become a Red Cross nurse because her father was in Cochin China, "officier, tu sais," she confided. There was too much excitement to sleep. It was a hot night with a radiant moon. Only a fortnight ago I had crossed to Le Touquet in a very different spirit. "Lights out" there now. Every station we passed was closely guarded by troops—soldiers patrolled the platforms and looked strange in the moonlight. "Ah! regardez celui-la," said the girl. "Il a l'air d'un Cosaque." "Plutôt d'un cuisinier," was the retort. A lot of chaff flew about. Someone asked for an egg as he was hungry. "Donnez moi des œufs, nous donnerons les coquilles à Guillaume." A man ran along the corridor excitedly and said the Germans had been sticking maps on the back of the "Potage Maggi" advertisements! "And the French have only just found this out," growled the airman. At Amiens we had to change, and I parted from my company for a more sleepy milieu. It was 5 o'clock in the morning when we rolled into Paris, a 15 hours' journey from London.

Paris was full of tension. One realized what the meaning of the war was to the French. On August 9 nearly all the shops were shut. Tricolour flags waved the length of the streets. There were no outside cafés, no outside shopping. No one was allowed in or out of Paris before 6 a.m. or after 6 p.m. I went to the Red Cross offices in the Rue François Premier and was received with the greatest courtesy by the Comtesse d'Haussonville and her daughter, Madame de Bonneval.

They asked me where I would like to go. Would I like to stay in hospital in Paris? I said I would like to go to the north—Lille, Arras, or perhaps Dunkirk. They said I must get a permit from the Minister of War to serve in a French military hospital. No foreigners as a rule, were allowed to do this.

The British Ambassador took me to the Ministry of War, and M. Messimy, who was at that time Minister of War, broke every regulation in my favour, gave me a permit, and expressed devoted gratitude for my services!

I went back to the Red Cross offices to buy my uniform. They were expecting a telegram every moment as to where I should be sent. News came through that the English troops were landing quietly and expeditiously in France.

Rumours of French successes in Alsace were flying about. No one had begun to take the Germans very seriously. At 6 o'clock in the evening Madame Jean de Castellane called at the British Embassy and said that a contingent of the French Red Cross had been wired for to go to Brussels and would I care to go with them? If so, I must be ready in two hours, dressed in my uniform, take a grip sack and leave the rest of my luggage behind. This, of course, I readily agreed to, and left at night with a party of French *infirmières* amongst whom was Comtesse Jacqueline de Pourtalès, who was a great friend and comfort all the time we were together. It was a long weary night journey. We took thirteen hours to accomplish what was usually done in four. Early on the morning of August 11 we crossed the Belgian frontier in a special train. We met with most touching enthusiasm; on the station platforms everyone seemed in tears but struggling to be brave. At Mons there was quite a large contingent of Belgian Red Cross to cheer us. It was a brilliant August morning. The country was all green and golden in the sunshine. The corn was waiting for the harvesters. I saw a few men in uniform reaping, but others were cutting down hedges or making trenches, or criss-crossing the fields with barbed wire. I longed to send out regiments of people to garner that corn before war had it trampled under foot.

No news, only rumour. The Belgians said that the English had landed at Antwerp—that Liége had not fallen. All this seemed incredible. My thoughts were in England. I could with difficulty keep back my tears. What were they doing in England, what were they planning? We were to be in Brussels in an hour, and I knew that my tears would soon dry under the stress and strain of work.

On August 15 Brussels seemed to me an amazing city. None of that feeling of tension that one had in Paris—still the outside cafés, still the open shops—and strangely enough, crowds of men in the streets. Belgium did not give the impression to the outward eye of a fighting nation; war might have been a million miles away save for the quaintly-dressed troops parading the streets. In the days between August 11 and August 15 I discovered that our contingent of French Red Cross was not much needed in Brussels. Brussels seemed supplied with thousands of beds in ambulances and hospitals, and Baron Lambert had a fully-equipped hospital with English nurses from Guy's. The chief surgeon, Dr. Depage, of Brussels, was very anxious to get some small ambulances of English nurses to send to the provinces, and having given my resignation from the French Red Cross organization in Brussels to Comte d'Haussonville, who came up from Paris to arrange certain difficulties, and was more than charming in his acquiescence, I wired to England for a surgeon and eight trained nurses to go to Namur, and also for funds to run the " Millicent Sutherland Ambulance." I hoped the English Red Cross would have been able to supply the nurses; but that was not possible.

I was now taking work under the Belgian " Service de Santé de l'Armée." I had instructions to ask my

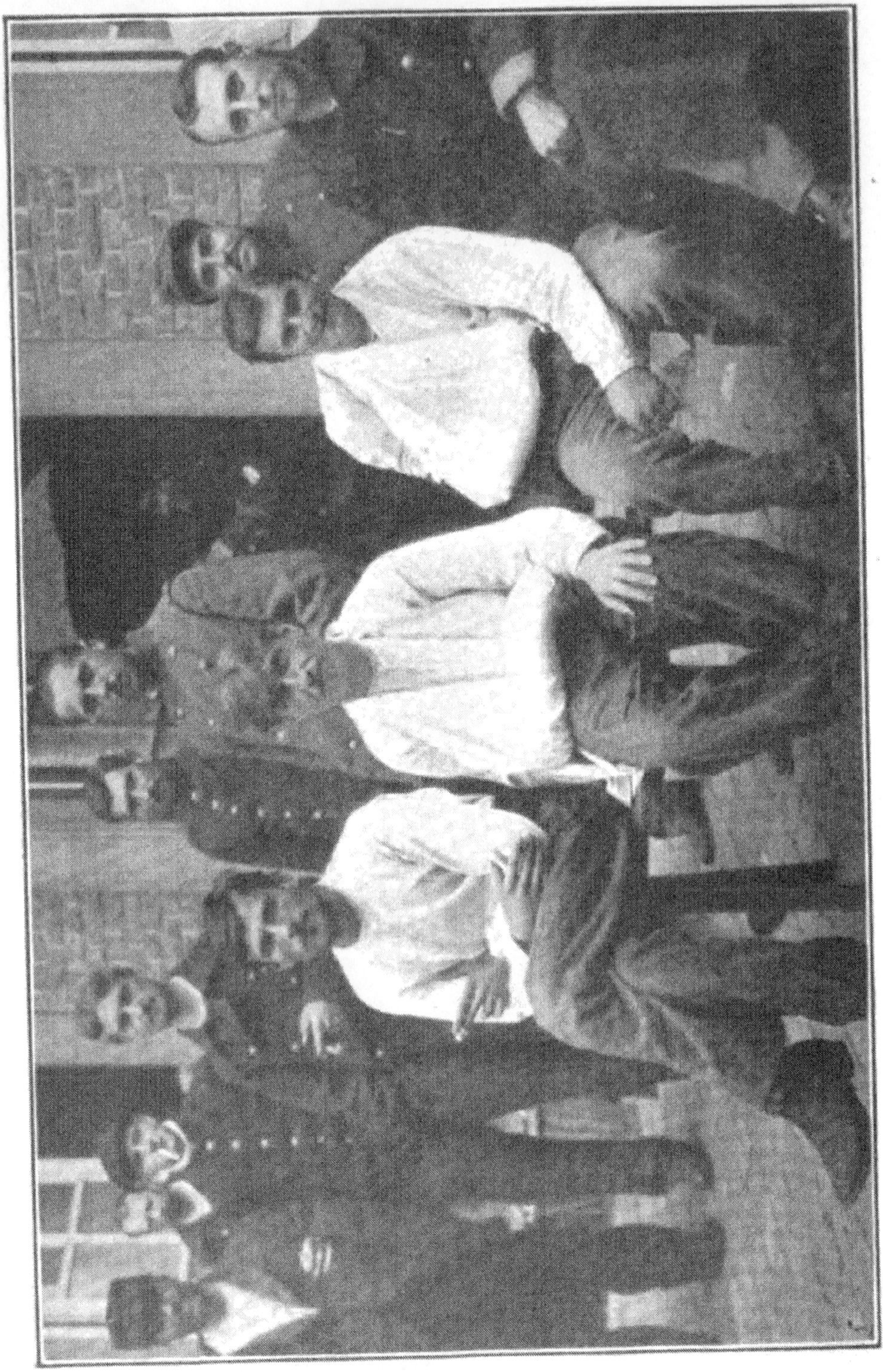

ambulance to come out at once, as communications were likely to be cut, and I took the opportunity of motoring to Namur to settle our dwelling. After obtaining the necessary permit from Headquarters our motor dashed out of Brussels and we soon struck the main road to Namur, which is some 50k. south. Every three or four miles the Gardes Civiques stopped us to examine passports and *cartes d'identité*, but in time we learnt to whisper the password of the day, "Gand," as we hurried on. The Belgians had erected amusing barricades of empty tramcars and trees and boughs to pull up the motors trying to go at a big speed. We passed charming little country places in the outskirts of Brussels; all of these had been converted into expectant ambulances and were flying the Red Cross flag. We drove through the beautiful Forêt de Soignes and I prayed that the Germans would not burn it down as in 1870 they had burnt the Bois de Boulogne.

There seemed to be a general impression that the Germans would take a turn through Brussels and avoid fortified cities like Namur so as not to waste time in getting on to France. This was what the brave Belgians said, but it was difficult to know much in that hour before the storm. A Frenchman told me he had seen a number of English troops near the Belgian frontier between Aulnoye and Mons. He said he knew they were English, because they were washing their faces and combing their hair. Aulnoye is a good way from Namur. At Wavre our motor broke down and we had to get another. The people ran out to tell us that they had taken a German prisoner, and they brought out a cavalryman's overcoat belonging to a trooper in the Queen Wilhelmina Regiment. The country people were trying on the coat and making jokes in Walloon. They gave me a German bullet out of the pocket as a souvenir. They cried, "Les Allemands sont des brutes et des assassins." It seemed to me all rather ghastly.

Great excitement about the arrival of twelve thousand troops from Algeria; "Les Turcos et les Zouaves sont dilettantes en baïonnette," they said. When we reached Namur in the wake of a motor which carried "*The Times*, London," written largely on it, we found most truly the atmosphere of war. Namur held one of the Etat-Majors of the Belgian Army. The garrison appeared grateful for the prospect of an English surgeon. Our ambulance was established in the convent of "Les Sœurs de Notre Dame."

Namur is a quiet provincial town, and a stronghold of the Catholic party. It stands on the junction of the river Meuse and the river Sambre; the "unhappy Sambre" I have christened it. All the bridges over the Meuse and over the railway were guarded and seemed ready to be blown up at any moment. The whole place was in a state of military expectancy. The Belgian troops were busy digging trenches and laying barbed wire. Namur is surrounded by nine forts, most of them from four to six kilometres away from the town on the heights. Fort Suarlée, Fort Emines, and Fort de Cognelée are north of Namur. Fort Marchevolette, Fort Maizeret, and Fort d'Andoy are east of Namur. Fort de Dave and Fort de St. Héribert are to the south, and Fort de Malomme is to the west.

On the way to Namur I saw distantly the historic field of Waterloo. The shades of dead warriors seemed to dance in the heat haze round the lion on the hill. I remembered that at Wavre Grouchy had lost his way and thus the battle to Napoleon. There was no food at Wavre when I was there. All the troops marching through had taken it, but there were little statues of Napoleon in all the shop windows. When I got back to Brussels I drank a " petit verre of Mandarin Napoléon " with a queer feeling that everything that has happened or is going to happen had happened before—sans motors et sans aeroplanes—and " après le temps de souffler " will happen again, as long as men continue to inhabit the earth and put their rights before their renunciations.

CHAPTER II.

IN WAR-SWEPT BELGIUM.

Namur During the Siege.

IT made me cross to see so many men loafing in the streets in Brussels. In fact, Brussels might almost have been called festive. I thought of the Duchess of Richmond's ball the night before Waterloo nearly 100 years ago. I should like to have taken those men and sent them out to carry the corn which was being left so imperturbably to its fate.

The Red Cross organization in Brussels I found to be very active and Dr. Depage a man to brush away all red tape and ineptitude. I could not help feeling that there was work ahead for us in the dark days to come. I was wiring all day at the expense of the Belgian Government to try to get money; the response was splendid, but I felt I should want more before the war was over. In Brussels I was immensely struck by the usefulness of the Boy Scouts. I felt very proud of the organization. They were more numerous than in Paris, though they do good work there.

On August 14 some French airmen came into the city and received a great ovation. Although the Belgians seemed lighthearted, they were evidently full of hope and determination, and I was much impressed by their fortitude. At the Legation Sir Francis Villiers and Miss Villiers were cheerful and calm. They could give very little news and there seemed little news in *The Times*, a copy of which I saw at the Legation. It was admitted now that Liége was in the hands of the Germans, but it was impossible to believe all the hideous stories of destruction and rapine floating around. I must say that Sir Francis Villiers discounted these largely. Still our hearts were utterly with the Belgians and their fight for independence.

The previous night at 10 o'clock a string of French Dragoon remounts were detrained at the Gare du Midi and were greeted with a volley of cheers. A few French officers, Chasseurs d'Afrique, in pale blue tunics and red breeches were with them. There was a queer atmosphere of excitement emanating from the groups that stood around. "Vive la France!" "Vive la Belgique!" they cried. I longed for one khaki-clad Tommy to walk in to make them cry " Vive l'Angleterre." When the little French airman was off again all our heads were out of the window, for some one said they had heard the boom of cannon, while another whispered " the Germans may be in Brussels to-night." I heard the Germans had five Army Corps advancing on Belgium, one or two suggested more. " They shoot badly, over your head or into your feet," said a Belgian soldier consolingly.

Next morning all Brussels was humming " La Brabançonne," for there was news of two small victories against the Germans at Haelen and at Eghezée. I went round to have a talk with Baron Lambert, the big Belgian banker. In his house I found the Belgian Minister from Berlin, Baron Beyens. He had had a difficult journey from Berlin, the women making themselves more objectionable than the men, putting their tongues out at him and screaming " Deutschland, Deutschland über Alles." Baron Beyens said he had spoken with Herr von Jagow, the German Foreign Minister, who was " frantic with the Belgians and their behaviour at Liège." But Beyens had answered, " How would you have expected us to act if the French had done as you have done ? " I thought Beyens seemed very depressed. He begged every one not to underrate the numerical strength of the German Army.

I met an unhappy British officer recovering from a bruised mouth. He had had very bad luck. A Belgian took him for a German prisoner, and hit him in the face. That, in the early days, was the worst of khaki.

That morning Sir William Lever cabled me £200 for my ambulance, and I went out to his soap-works in the outskirts of Brussels to fetch the money. The afternoon was bathed in sunshine. The river Senne was sparkling in the heat. Beyond the poplars, which quivered above the old barges on the river, was a nursery garden full of roses, phlox, daisies, and carnations, and white, happy butterflies flitting above them. What would flowers and butterflies matter to many when this war was over? I looked up into the sky where the sun was going down a golden ball in the west, and I saw a German "Taube" hovering over the city. In a few moments it was gone. At first the Belgian soldiers let off their rifles at these aeroplanes, but later on an order came out against such a useless waste of ammunition.

On August 16 my eight nurses and my surgeon arrived in Brussels. To them and to their skill and courage I have dedicated this book. I went to meet them at the station, and when I returned to the hotel I was told that the line had been blown up between Brussels and Namur. It was absolutely essential that we should get to Namur at all costs, so I went off to the "Inspecteur-Général du Service de Santé de l'Armée," for he alone in all Brussels seemed to be at the end of a telephone. He rang up Namur and found that the direct route from Brussels to Namur could no longer be traversed. A bomb had fallen on the station at Namur out of an aeroplane twenty minutes after I had left the station two days previously. Now the Germans had been trying to blow up the station at Gembloux, on the direct line between Namur and Brussels. However, they said that if we started early in the morning we could reach Namur by a roundabout route through Charleroi. The next morning we were off. At Charleroi we were told the train could only go as far as Moustiers, because the woods were full of Germans. Still good fortune favoured us, for when we reached Moustiers they said, " All right ahead," and we came straight on by train to Namur.

There are coalfields and a pretty thick manufacturing population between Charleroi and Namur. The line was strongly protected by troops, and outside one station I saw a squadron of French Dragoons. Their shiny helmets were covered by khaki bags, which looked quaint. They were the first French troops on active service in Belgium I had seen.

The Convent of Namur after last week's hurry seemed extraordinarily quiet. Les Sœurs de Notre Dame are scholastic sisters, and they had arranged the school part of the building, which was new and sanitary, as a hospital. My nurses were given a long dormitory where the scholars usually sleep and I had a small dormitory to myself. The nuns treated us most kindly, and said they would do all the cooking for the wounded. "Mais il n'y a pas encore des blessés," they said thankfully. In Namur communications were cut. Even the English motor-car with the photographers, who had caught us unawares, had slipped off. There appeared to be no English in Namur except one young lady, Miss Louise Grabowski, who did good work at the Red Cross. In the Belgian Red Cross ambulances and in the military hospital all the nursing is done by partly trained, but willing, nuns and ladies. The dressings are done by the doctors. A rumour reached us of a big fight at Dinant on the Meuse, south of Namur. Two companies of French infantry had been cut up, as the French artillery did not get there in time. At night when I was going to bed I heard the Convent bell ring loudly and one of the nuns fetched me down and said some gentlemen wished to speak to me. Below I found my friend Count Jean Cornet d'Elzius, who had brought me to Namur and was looking after the Belgian Provincial Ambulances, and an English surgeon and dresser of the English Red Cross party who had come out to Brussels. The surgeon said they had found in Brussels, just as we had, too many helpers, and no one else needed there, so they were going to the battlefields. " Your hospital of 150 beds here will be very useful," he said, and then added gravely, " We saw a lot of dead Germans to-day." I felt anxious about these doctors, because they were dressed in khaki like combatant officers, and Count Jean Cornet, their Belgian companion, was full of pluck. I heard that an hour after they had left the Convent they were caught by the Germans and taken as prisoners to Hamburg.

It was a strange experience next morning to be sitting in the old Convent garden full of fruit trees and surrounded by high walls, whilst the nuns, the novices, and the postulants flitted about the paths with their rosaries and their little books. It was almost impossible to realize that there were nearly 200 nuns in the Convent so quietly did they move. From an upper window the nurses and I watched a regiment of Belgian artillery roll by. It was coming in from the country. " A big battle rages near Ramillies," said one nun. " All the poor families are coming in in carts." The Belgian military doctor, Dr. Cordier, came to inspect our hospital equipment, which only arrived by the last train that reached Namur. I always wonder what happened to Dr. Cordier afterwards. He went away with the Staff. I hope I shall see him again. He criticized our carbolic, smiled at the glycerine for the hands, and was immensely impressed by our instruments. He told me it was a "jour de repos," that the French cavalry had travelled at least 100 kilometres yesterday, and were as tired as the Germans! A great many of the ambulances here had been up to now filled with "tired men." "Ils sont trop vite fatigués," he said.

It was almost impossible to find out what was really going on. The noise of the motors, the scout motor cyclists, and the occasional whirr of an aeroplane mingled their sounds with a perpetual clanging of church bells. Our nurses were all busy making splints, cushions, sand-bags, &c., and generally getting this scholastic side of the nunnery into one of the finest hospitals in Belgium. The English nuns helped us very much. I shall always remember Sister Marie des Cinq Anges and Sister Bernard. Yesterday the Prince de Chimay came through with a mitrailleuse on a motor. "That fellow will be killed for sure," they said. After he had passed, a few tired Belgian soldiers came straggling in with another mitrailleuse on a country cart. When a terrific rain-storm had passed over, we, in spite of distant firing, visited the military hospital, an uncomfortable place, with nuns of the Hospice de S. Louis for nurses, and good military surgeons, who assured us that they were building a new military hospital to be ready in two years! They must have good constitutions, these Belgians, to stand what is done to them. One old man of sixty-eight had both his legs amputated, a bomb had shattered them—the bomb I had so narrowly escaped at Namur the other day. Two aviator officers were broken-limbed from a heavy fall from their aeroplane. One cheery French soldier had six bullets in him. He laughed, "Il ne me manque que la septième pour me donner de la chance."

I saw six wounded Uhlans—German prisoners. The surgeon asked me to tell them he would give them open postcards to write to their people. This seemed to please them. I asked them why they were fighting. "Because the English have taken all our ships" said one. "But why are you fighting the Belgians?" "Ah, that we do not know," he replied, "Our officers tell us to." One man came from Berlin, one from Hamburg, one from Schleswig, and two of them were boys of nineteen.

On August 21 there was almost a panic in Namur. All night long the guns had been firing from the forts, and all the morning there was that hurrying and scurrying into groups of weeping hatless women and of little children. The great secrecy as to all events that were passing filled them with untold fear.

It was evidently the beginning of a terrible experience. The Germans had been massing on the left bank of the Meuse and had come as close to Namur as circumstances would permit. They had passed through the country carrying off the cattle, burning the villages, cutting the telegraph and telephone wires, and attacking the railway stations. The closeness of the atmosphere had made Namur almost impossible to breathe in, that day. Tired Belgian soldiers came in. They seemed to have so much to wear and to carry. A regiment of Congolais, a Foreign Legion which had been in service in the Congo, marched through with their guns drawn by dogs. The place was full of refugees who had been brought in from the country in carts. The Germans had burnt the villages of Ramillies and Petit Rosière. The inhabitants had been driven for shelter to Namur with a few poor bundles. They could not be kept at Namur for fear of shortage of food, so they were sent on to Charleroi. One little post boy had lain for three hours in a trench while the shells rained with deadly fire over him. He escaped without a scratch. In the morning at 7.30 a bomb had been dropped from an aeroplane a few streets from our Convent. It was intended to fall in the Jesuit College, which was temporarily used as

Artillery barracks, but it missed the college and dropped near the Academy of Music, breaking all the windows, ploughing a hole in the ground, and badly wounding four artillerymen. A soldier came by me leading a horse. He was crying bitterly. It was strange to see. He had just heard that his brother had been killed.

A rumour reached us that the Germans were already in Brussels. Certainly the Court and Legations had moved to Antwerp and the protection of her forts. At the provisional barracks opposite the Convent there had been great excitement. A whole Belgian regiment had departed suddenly in motor-cars, and a crowd of women cheered them, with tears streaming down their faces. They never came back. At 12 o'clock the sky became very gloomy, and one of the nuns gave me a bit of glass to look through at the partial eclipse of the sun. About seven-tenths of the sun's face was obscured. This eclipse seemed to add to the awfulness of the situation.

We went over to the Café des Quatre Fils d'Aymond for our two franc dinner, as we used to do every day. There we found a man discoursing eloquently on the attack on the station at Gembloux by the Germans, and of its defence. We listened for a long time until we heard the explosion of another bomb in the next street. People were rushing hither and thither in a distracted manner, but no one could say who had been killed. At the door of the café we looked up, and I saw the Hornet of Hell, as I call the German "Taube" which had dropped the bomb, floating slowly away. I thought it better to get my nurses to the shelter of the Convent, as German shells directed upon the station were beginning to fly over the town. We heard the long screaming whistle as they rushed through the air like some stupendous firework, and the distant explosion. Some Belgian soldiers came up and asked "Where were the English ?" I placed them at Louvain, at Tirlemont, or close to Namur—100,000 of them, I said wildly. I wished most heartily I had known where they were. It was absolutely necessary to keep up the spirits of the people. Their hopeless dejection since the German shelling began was too terrible to behold. We received no letters or papers, but the little Namur rag *L'Ami de l'Ordre* told us calmly about passing events. "On ne doit pas s'en inquiéter ni s'en affoler !"

On August 22 I wrote my diary in the cellars of the convent. We had taken refuge there with all the schoolchildren, who were very frightened. We sat among sacks of flour, which the military authorities had put in charge of the nuns. Our nurses cut out red flannel bed-jackets and tried to take photographs ! The German shells had been whistling ominously over the

Convent for 24 hours. They said they were directed against the fort of Maizeret. Rumour had it that Fort Marchevolette had fallen. Anyway, three of the turrets had been put out of action. Five thousand French had been hurried through the city as a relief force at 7 o'clock in the morning. They said they would have been of more use the previous day, August 21. The Bishop came to see the Reverend Mother. She assured us he was full of courage. He had seen General Michel, the Commander of the Forts, in whom hope ran high. On the other hand, they told us thousands of Germans surrounded Namur, but the tales were as numerous as the shells, and one listened to everything knowing that knowledge as to the real military tactics would never be given to us. Poor little Belgians! They were brave enough and tried hard to repress their panic. Personally my longing was for a Highland Brigade to march into the town. I was so tired of the discouraging refrain "Où sont les Anglais?"

One of the strangest parts of all was the fact that we were nursing in the Convent of *Les Sœurs de Notre Dame de Namur*. Exactly 100 years ago the Venerable Foundress, Mother Julie Billiart, who called herself Sister Ignatius, wrote her experiences of the Napoleonic War in this same Convent.

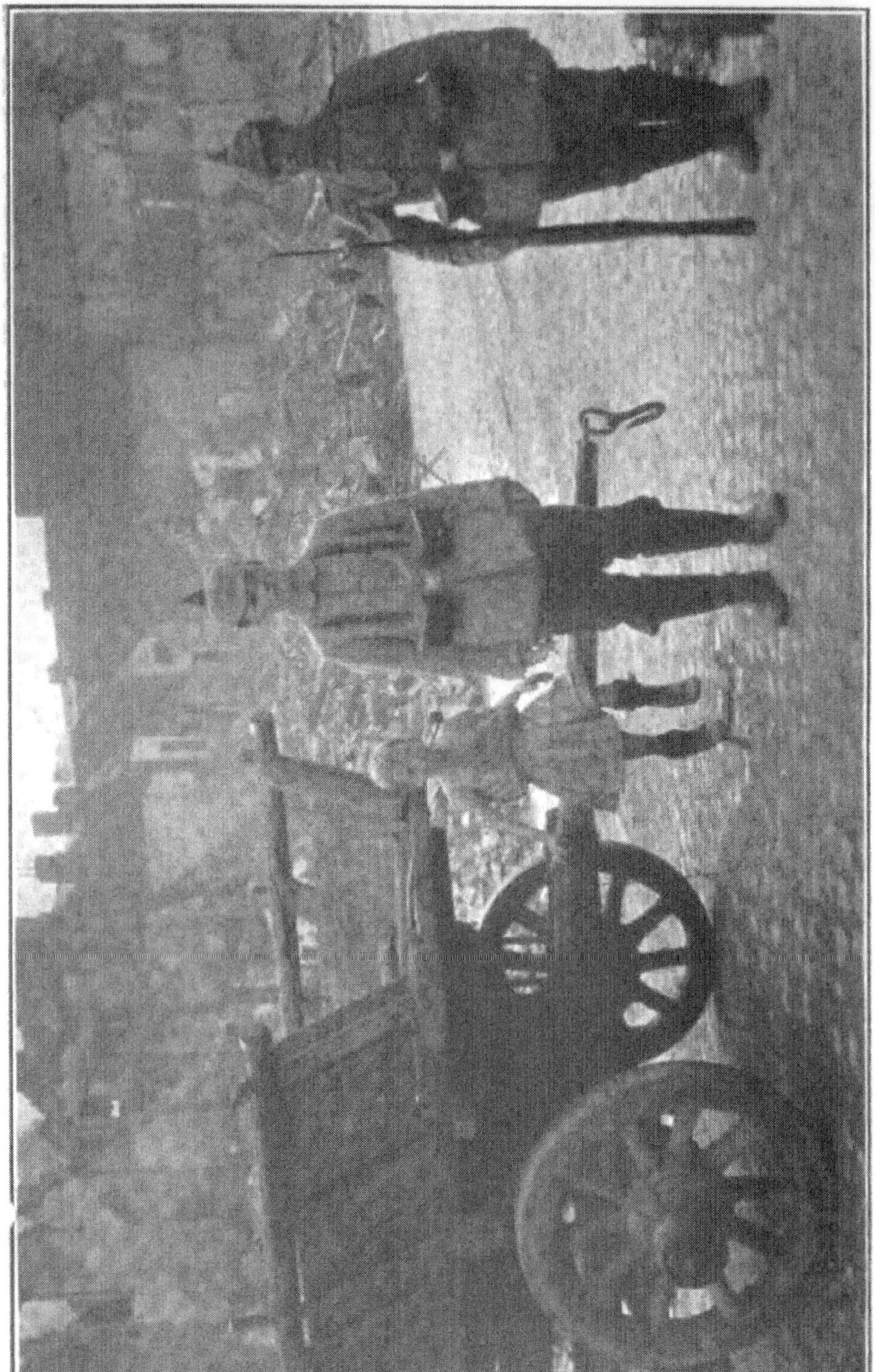

"My daughter, pay no heed to these rumours of war. We have our great Patroness, our good and tender Mother, to watch over us. Put your trust in her and no harm will come to you. If God is for us, who shall be against us? People have tried to frighten us here at Namur as elsewhere, but we have placed all our confidence in the Lord. We keep very quiet. We pray as much as we can."

During these days of penury and distress no one knew how the Venerable Mother contrived to feed her sisters and children. In the same mysterious way to-day the Reverend Mother contrived to feed the soldiers and children, her 200 nuns, and novices and postulants, and has promised to feed our wounded. One finds in Mother Julie Billiart's record of devotion and of difficulties overcome many allusions to the War of 1814-1815. The allied armies were overrunning Belgium. Jumet, Gembloux, Fleurus, were then almost the scene of war—as they are indeed actually the scene of war to-day. As in this August, 1914, so a hundred years ago the Sambre and the Meuse formed the line of separation between the opposing forces before the memorable battle of Waterloo—or, as the nuns called it, "la Bataille de Mont St. Jean." Namur, too, was cut off. The record of the troops retreating after Waterloo might have been the report of a War

Correspondent of events in Belgium to-day with simply a change of alliances, so marvellously has history repeated itself.

After the defeat of Napoleon's grand army at Ligny nearly all that was left of it, to the number of 40,000, poured into Namur on June 19, 1815. Early the next day the Prussians were at the gates of the city. All day firing went on. No cannon, however, was used. The French had not more than two pieces—the Prussians had plenty, but the commander was generous enough to abstain from bombarding the town, which would soon have been reduced to ashes. The Allies entered at 6 in the evening by one gate—while the French retreated at the opposite one.

Mother Julie writes in her diary :—" The community of Gembloux was thrown into consternation by seeing the farms around them all on fire and cannon balls flying through the air. The day after the great battle the French troops came pouring into the town of Namur. It was Sunday morning and they were hoping to be left in peace, when a terrific noise was heard. The soldiers were breaking in the doors and windows of the Abbey and beginning to pillage the place. The pupils, who were all with us at the time, screamed and shrieked with terror. We took them up to the top of the house and sent to the commander for a guard. The Frenchmen left without doing any harm, but were succeeded by the Prussians, driven to desperation by three days' fighting, and prepared to pillage in their turn, and were only prevented from doing so by our guard."

Truly this valiant little country has been the cockpit of war from century to century, and Namur has been taken and retaken so often that her foundations have perpetually been renewed.

To-day the Sisters of Notre Dame de Namur number nearly 4,000. In Belgium they have 40 convents, besides the Mother Convent of Namur, and in America 42, in Great Britain 19, in the Belgian Congo two, in Rhodesia two, and in the Orange Free State one.

CHAPTER III.

DAYS AND NIGHTS OF HORROR AT NAMUR.

HERE is an extract from my diary of August 23:—

"NAMUR.

"Never shall I forget the afternoon of August 22. The shelling of the past hours having suddenly ceased, I went to my dormitory. I had had practically no rest for two nights, and after the emotions of the morning I was falling asleep when Sister Kirby rushed into my room, calling out, 'Sister Millicent! the wounded!'

"I rushed down the stone stairs. The wounded, indeed! Six motor-cars and as many waggons were at the door, and they were carrying in those unhappy fellows. Some were on stretchers, others were supported by willing Red Cross men. One or two of the stragglers fell up the steps from fatigue and lay there. Many of these men had been for three days without food or sleep in the trenches.

"In less than 20 minutes we had 45 wounded on our hands. A number had been wounded by shrapnel, a few by bullet wounds, but luckily some were only wounded by pieces of shell. These inflict awful gashes, but if they are taken in time the wounds rarely prove mortal.

"The wounded were all Belgian—Flemish and Walloon —or French. Many were Reservists. Our young surgeon, Mr. Morgan, was perfectly cool and so were our nurses. What I thought would be for me an impossible task became absolutely natural: to wash wounds, to drag off rags and clothing soaked in blood, to hold basins equally full of blood, to soothe a soldier's groans, to raise a wounded man while he was receiving extreme unction, hemmed in by nuns and a priest, so near he seemed to death; these actions seemed suddenly to become an insistent duty, perfectly easy to carry out.

"All the evening the wounded and the worn out were being rushed in. If they had come in tens one would not have minded, but the pressure of cases to attend to was exhausting. One could not refuse to take them, for they said there were 700 in the military hospital already, while all the smaller Red Cross ambulances were full.

"So many of the men were in a state of prostration bordering almost on dementia, that I seemed instantly enveloped in the blight of war. I felt stunned—as if I were passing through an endless nightmare. Cut off as we were from all communication with the outer world, I realized what a blessing our ambulance was to Namur. I do not know what the nuns would have done without our nurses at such a moment. No one, until these awful things happen, can conceive the untold value of fully-trained and disciplined British nurses. The nuns were of great use to us, for they helped in every possible tender way, and provided food for the patients. The men had been lying in the trenches outside the forts. Hundreds of wounded, we believed, were still waiting to be brought in, and owing to the German cannonading it was impossible to get near them. I kept on thinking and hoping that the allied armies must be coming to the rescue of Namur."

"LATER.

"The guns never cease. They say the heavy French artillery arrived last night, and have taken up the work of the Marchevolette fort, which is reported to be out of action, but one of our wounded tells us that this artillery came 24 hours too late. and that the French force on the Meuse is not sufficient. The Belgian Gendarmerie have just been in and collected all arms and ammunition. I have been seeking for the rosaries the patients carry in their purses. They want to hold them in their hands or have them slung round their necks. On the floor there is a confusion of uniforms, képis, and underclothing, which the nuns are trying to sort. It looks a hopeless occupation. Our surgeon is busy in the operating theatre, cutting off a man's fingers; he was the first to be brought in and had his right hand shattered."

"Sunday, August 23.

"There is a dreadful bombardment going on. Some of our wounded who can walk wrap themselves in blankets and go to the cellars. Nothing that I could say would stop them. They are fresh from the trenches. Luckily we are in a new fire-proof building, and I must stay with my sick men who cannot move. The shells sing over the convent from the deep booming German guns—a long singing scream and then an explosion which seems only a stone's throw away. The man who received extreme unction the night before is mad with terror. I do not believe that he is after all so badly wounded. He has a bullet in his shoulder, and it is not serious. He has lost all power of speech, but I believe that he is an example of what I have read of and what I had never seen—a man dying of sheer fright.

"The nurses and one or two of the nuns are most courageous and refuse to take shelter in the cellars, which are full of the novices and schoolchildren. The electric and gas supplies have been cut off. The only lights we have to use are a few hand lanterns and nightlights. Quite late in the afternoon we heard a tremendous explosion. The Belgian had blown up the new railway bridge, but unfortunately there are others by which the Germans can cross, and presently we hear that they are in the town. There is some rapid fusillading through the streets and two frightened old Belgian officers run into the convent and ask for Red Cross bands, throwing down their arms and maps. In a few minutes, however, they regained self control and went out in the streets without the Red Cross bands. Heaven knows what happened to them.

"Now the German troops are fairly marching in. I hear them singing as they march. They sing wonderfully—in parts as if well trained for this singing. It seems almost cowardly to write this, but for a few minutes there was relief to see them coming and to feel that this awful firing would soon cease. On they march! Fine well-set-up men with grey uniforms. They have stopped shooting now. I see them streaming into the market-place. A lot of stampeding artillery horses gallop by with Belgian guns. On one of the limbers still lay all that was left of a man. It is too terrible. What can these brave little people do against this mighty force? Some of the

Germans have fallen out and are talking to the people in the streets. These are so utterly relieved at the cessation of the bombardment that in their fear they are actually welcoming the Germans. I saw some women press forward and wave their handkerchiefs.

"Suddenly upon this scene the most fearful shelling begins again. It seemed almost as if the guns were in the garden. Mr. Morgan, Mr. Winser, and I were standing there. I had just buried my revolver under an apple tree when the bombardment began once more. The church bells were clanging for vespers. Then whizz! bang! come the shells over our heads again. Picric acid and splinters fall at our very feet. We rush back into the convent, and there are fifteen minutes' intense and fearful excitement while the shells are crashing into the market-place. We see German soldiers running for dear life. Can it be the French artillery that is driving them out? There is clang-clanging at the convent bell. Women half fainting, and wounded, old men and boys are struggling in. Their screams are dreadful. They had all gone into the Grande Place to watch the German soldiers marching, and were caught in this sudden firing. A civilian wounded by a shell in the stomach was brought into the Ambulance. He died in 20 minutes. We can only gather incoherent accounts from these people as to what had happened.

The Germans sounded the retreat and the shelling seemed to stop. At last it leaks out that the German troops on the other side of the town did not know that their own troops had crossed the Meuse on the opposite side. They were firing on the Citadel, an antiquated fort of no value. The shells fell short, and before the Germans discovered their mistake they had killed many of their own soldiers and Belgian civilians who had rushed up to see the German troops. It seems a horrible story, but absolutely true.

"Now it is quiet again, save for the sighs of the suffering. All night long we hear the tramp, tramp, tramp, of German infantry in the streets, their words of command, their perpetual deep-throated songs. They are full of swagger, and they are very anxious to make an impression upon the Belgians—to cow them in fact—these Belgians so used to peaceful country-sides and simple useful employments. Our wounded are doing well, and one must remember that, if their nerves have gone to pieces, to lie in trenches with this awful artillery fire bursting over them, knowing that even if they lifted their heads a few inches it might be blown off, must be an appalling sensation. The Germans hate hand to hand encounters, but they love to manipulate cannon that can blow you to pieces at a distance of six miles. If one believes the Belgian soldiers, apart from artillery work the Germans shoot badly and in a very odd position with their rifles resting on their hips and their heads protected by one arm as they lie on the ground; their firing must be very wild. A Belgian soldier told me that the Germans have a second line behind the first line, called " watchers," who do not fire on the enemy at all, but simply watch the men in front to see that they are doing their duty properly and never let a man fall out.

"The Doctor and I went up into the tower in the dark. The bombardment had ceased, but everywhere on the horizon there were blazing fires, villages and country mansions flaring in the darkness. Motor-cars dashed past. Instead of Belgian, one sees now only German motors filled with German officers. Where are the English and the big French troops ? That is what I am wondering. And what is the end to be ? "

In my diary on August 23, 1914, I have written what I considered the most awful experience of my life, but last night, August 24, there was another climax, and I hope I shall never live through such a night again.

The day was peaceful enough after the previous soul-stirring hours. The man who had lost his voice was beginning to whisper. All he could say was, " J'ai peur, j'ai peur." These words seem ordinary words from a child or a woman, but they were terrible coming perpetually from a strong man under such circumstances. One gathered from them an idea of the horrors he must have seen and heard. The wounded gave me terrible accounts of the new German siege guns. When the shell explodes it bursts everything to smithereens inside the forts. The men who are not killed and wounded become utterly demoralized and hysterical, even mad, in awful apprehension of the next shot. They say the Namur forts were jerry-built and absolutely unreliable. The Germans declare that they destroyed one fort at Liège with a single shot of this siege cannon. They have a range of at least 16 kilometres (ten miles). The Germans say 24 (15 miles), but then they are boastful.

Early in the afternoon a German Count with a Red Cross on his arm came and inspected our ambulance at the convent. He was perfectly civil, and one had to be civil in return. He drank the beer which the nuns tremblingly pressed upon him, and took a note of the sacks of flour which the nuns were keeping in the cellars.

" Pour l'autorité militaire Belge ? " they said.

" Allemande," the young Count replied significantly.

Inwardly I made a mental note to get possession of that flour, for the German troops were rapidly depleting Namur of all its food, and refugees were streaming into the town. We had not seen butter, milk, or eggs for days. Now the nuns came to me and said there was no yeast for the bread, and they were trying various recipes to make bread without yeast. It sounded indigestible.

The German Count adopted a sort of "gnädigste Frau" (charming woman) manner to me, and paid compliments to English women; he seemed thoroughly pleased with himself. He said, "Now the Germans are in possession of Namur all will be quiet and well arranged. There will be no trouble unless the civilians are treacherous and fire on the soldiers. If they do that we shall set fire to the town." Having said this he clattered out. The Namuriens had suffered so much and had seemed so utterly broken down, it did not strike me that the civilians would venture to fire on these thousands of troops that were filling their streets, their barracks, and their shops. All I kept on thinking was, "Where are the English and the French?"

L'Ami de l'Ordre, the Namur paper, had been promptly secured by the Germans and only gave us exactly what the Germans told them to write. Some of the lightly wounded prisoners wanted the blood of the editor, and wrote frantic letters, which I had to confiscate, expressing their indignation at the new tone of their precious Press.

It was a hot, still summer night. We had begun to laugh again. We were so interested in our wounded. "Silly Billy," "Bonny Boy," "Baby boy"—they had all their nick-names—and we were so relieved at the cessation of firing save of one distant cannon which would not stop and was evidently attacking the last fort. It was 10 o'clock and I decided to go to bed and was nearly undressed when a few rifle shots rang out in the street near the convent. A pause, and then came a perfect fusillade of rifle shots. It was dreadful while it lasted. Had the Belgians disregarded the warning of the Town Council, of *L'Ami de l'Ordre*, and of the German "swankers," and refused to take their defeat lying down? Of course, if the civilians were firing, it was mad rashness. My door burst open and Mr. Winser, our stretcher-bearer, rushed in, calling out, "My God, Duchess, they have fired the town."

It is almost impossible to describe the scene that followed. The Hôtel de Ville was on fire, the market place was on fire, they said that the Arsenal was on fire, but I found that the powder magazine had been emptied long ago. Then came the message that the town was fired at the four corners. One of the buildings of the convent was absolutely fire-proof and in this portion the worn-out wounded were very quiet. We had about a hundred in a dormitory in an older building.

The flames simply shot up beside this and the sparks were falling about the roof. Fortunately the convent was all surrounded by a garden and the wind was blowing the flames away from us. The whole sky was illuminated; we came to the conclusion that there was nothing to do but to wait and watch the fire, and leave the patients alone until we saw the flames *must* reach us. It was a terrible hour. The nurses courageously re-assured the wounded and persuaded most of them to remain in bed.

My mind became a perfect blank. We had gone through so much that it was perfectly impossible to think of what was going to happen or of what had happened. I was wondering if we should have to leave the burning building and go out into the street, whether I had better dress again or keep on my pyjamas and pull my top boots over them—into such a silly condition does one's brain degenerate.

The Padre came in at last and said that the flames would not reach us. While we were all talking and wondering what would happen next, there was a violent ringing at the convent bell, then a banging at the door and a German voice ordering loudly, "Oeffnen! Oeffnen!" I persuaded one of the nuns to undo the latch and I and one or two of the nurses went out with Dr. Morgan. While we were struggling with the lock I felt as if I were actually *living* some book of adventure, such as I had read in my youth. The flames shooting into the sky, the smoke pouring over the convent, and, though the rifle firing had ceased, the distant booms of the cannon—And here were the Germans rattling at the door!

Outside was a smart motor-car full of soldiers armed to the teeth protecting a young German officer who was so like the Crown Prince that he might have been his brother. He was very cross and very nervous. He said he wanted to know the way to the Citadel. A nun whom I called out, said that the only way to the Citadel was past the Hôtel de Ville. He said he did not wish to go that way, for it was burning to a cinder. He looked at me and asked me to go with him and show him another way. But I stood my ground, and said I was a stranger and an Englishwoman and had never been to the Citadel in my life. So he spared me that unpleasant experience. He told me that some of the civilian inhabitants had been shooting at the soldiers from dark windows. He said that the whole town would be burnt. He seemed in a towering rage, and in a good fear, too. He said that, of course, all Red Cross people were safe and " always women." Then he drove away with his soldiers, perhaps to his death.

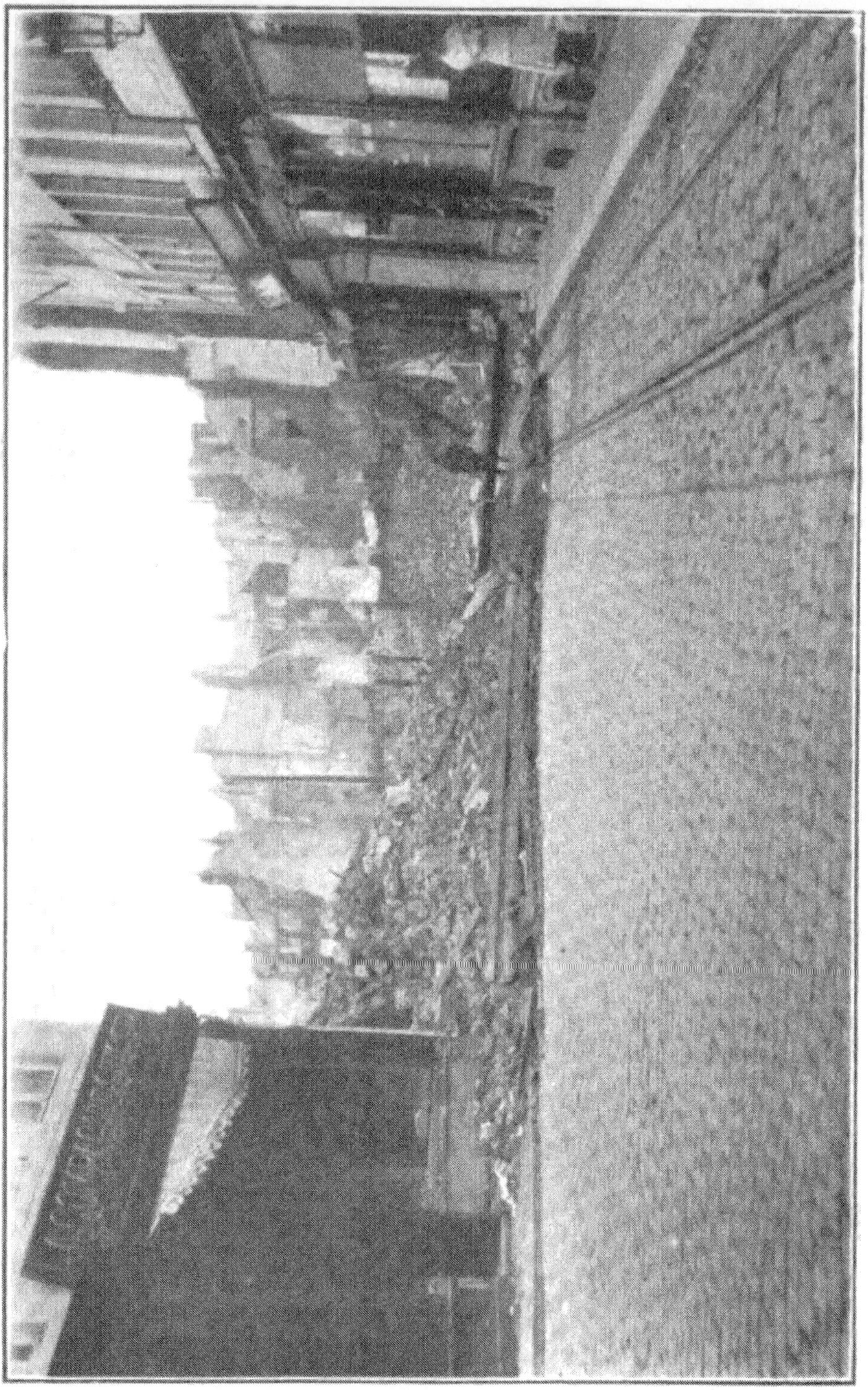

We were very fortunate at being on the Meuse side of the town. Though the fire had started there, the soldiers' barracks were in our direction and they certainly would put the flames out before they reached their quarters. Even now the Tocsin was ringing. It rang all night. When the danger of the fire became less we snatched a little sleep. I was very tired. When I awoke I heard that the Commander-General von Below had given an order to blow up houses to prevent the spread of the fire and the Fire Brigade was out with the hose.

In the afternoon we ventured into the smoky street. It was like walking through a dense fog. All the buildings were smouldering. The whole of the market-place and the Hôtel de Ville had been burnt and the dear little café where we went for our meals before the bombardment. All the shutters were up on the shops that had not been burnt and one could hardly walk for the number of German troops massed in the streets, bivouacking with their rifles stacked before them. The streets were practically impassable, but infantry battalions forced a way through artillery batteries, and hundreds and hundreds of motor transport waggons.

The Germans seemed to be doing the whole of this campaign on gasolene—that is to say, they use motor transport throughout, and they may, therefore, find themselves in difficulty when the roads are cut up and the rains come. Their transport is very perfect, but is too heavy and their supply of gasolene may fail them.

The doctor and I thought we had better visit the Commander, General von Below. The Germans were perfectly civil to us. Some of them spoke to us and said that they were marching on to Maubeuge in a few days, and that they had already invested Brussels. They seemed so absolutely sure of themselves that they still treated the English with politeness and were for the moment only terrorizing and bullying the Belgians. I have never yet been able to probe the mystery of the rapid fall of the Namur forts—I had been told they would hold out a month—I do not understand why the Belgian General Staff should have left the town 12 hours before the fall leaving the soldiers without any officers, but I had heard too much of the words "trahison" and "espionage," and I suppose the whole thing was wise strategy I think it was a good thing that Namur was a Clerical centre, because later the Commander took up his residence with the Bishop, and probably the Bishop restrained him from enforcing too harsh measures against the population. This, however, is only my surmise.

Herr General von Below and his smartly-uniformed officers received my card with great courtesy, and I began to see that it would be necessary to keep up this courtesy by a fixed determination on my part to get all I wanted.

The Headquarters Staff was established at the Hôtel de Hollande. The Germans were being importuned by residents asking various favours and questions. One Belgian lady asked if she might follow her husband, who was a prisoner, to Germany. "You may follow him if you like, madame," was the reply, "but you cannot accompany him." The lady looked very sorrowful.

General von Below apologized for receiving me in his bedroom, so terribly overflowing were all the other rooms with officers. Feld-Marschall von der Goltz, who arrived *en route* to take up his duties in Brussels, was kept waiting while the General spoke to me. I was merely introduced to this elderly gentleman of Turkish fame. He was buttoned up to his nose in an overcoat. Above the collar gleamed a pair of enormous glasses. He was covered with orders. He shook me by the hand, and went out.

I did not discuss the situation with General von Below. I took him for granted. He said he was sure he had met me at Homburg, and that he would arrange with one of the diplomats to get a telegram through to Berlin, which he trusted would be copied in the London papers, announcing the safety of our Ambulance.

"Accept my admiration for your work, Duchess," he said. He spoke perfect English. To accept the favours of my country's foe was a bad moment for me, but the Germans were in possession of Namur and I had to consider my hospital from every point of view. Also those who are of the Red Cross and who care for suffering humanity and for the relief of pain and sickness should strive to remember nothing but the heartache of the world and the pity of it.

General von Below "did me the honour" to call the next morning at our Ambulance. He was accompanied by Baron Kessler, his aide-de-camp, who composed the scenario of *La Légende de Josephe*. He had been much connected with Russian opera in London during the past season. It was exceedingly odd to meet him under such circumstances, after having so often discussed "art" with him in London.

I was able, with the assistance of Mr. Winser, our stretcher-bearer, whose sister had married a German, to obtain an order that the flour in the cellars might be kept for the use of our Ambulance. I left the order with the nuns; and I trust that all those sacks will be for the benefit of the poor of Namur and surrounding districts during the terrible trying winter which is before them. Our nurses continued to tend the patients and dress their wounds as if nothing had ever happened and they were in a hospital in London! How grateful those French and Belgians were to them! The Flemish were most amusing in their efforts to make us understand their language.

The women wounded patients gave us the most trouble. They cried and screamed all the time. The Germans had brought us in two more Belgian wounded soldiers; one very badly shot in the arm.

I went into the convent garden, so tired I was of the grey German troops, their songs, and their invasion of the streets. I was feeling horribly sad. Had the English and French been beaten? Why were there no English soldiers amongst our wounded? Was it really true that none of them had come into Belgium at all? I felt utterly cut off from the outside world. The Germans seemed so overwhelming at the first glance, so numerically appalling. There is an old legend that Namur never suffers too much injury from disaster owing to the special protection of the Virgin. Flowers bloom around her statue. Perhaps these beliefs are comforting. I suppose that it must have been under the influence of St. Julienne de Cornillon that I went to Namur. *She* said, "Let us go to Namur. It is the usual refuge of exiles!" If it were not for our wounded how quickly, if it were possible, would I escape!

CHAPTER IV.

LIFE AMONG THE INVADERS.

ON August 27 the Germans were in full possession of peaceful Namur. The last fort had fallen and the last Belgian wounded from the forts had been brought into our hospital. We had now over 100 patients. The Germans were occupying the temporary barracks across the road from the convent which had lately been full of Belgian soldiers. Some German Infantrymen brought us three wounded comrades—an artillery waggon had upset and passed over them. We took them in with our other patients. They were fatter and dirtier than the Belgians, and tattooed all over with most extraordinary pictures. They seemed pretty miserable and utterly tired out. What a change in three days! German sentries stood outside the military hospital, Germans filled every café, and up and down the streets there was a perpetual march of German soldiers.

There was a look of terror on each face amongst the inhabitants.

Poor Belgians! Was there no one to help them? The walls were pasted with German proclamations. For instance, owing to the shooting of the civilians an order came out that all soldiers, Belgian or French that might be hidden in the houses, were to be given up as prisoners of war before 4 o'clock in the afternoon in front of the prison. If this order were not obeyed the prisoners would be condemned to perpetual hard labour in Germany. If any arms were hidden in houses and were not given up by 4 o'clock the inhabitants would be shot. All streets would be occupied by German guards, who would take from each street ten male hostages. These hostages would be shot if any other person whosoever fired upon the German troops. No houses could be locked at night. After 8 o'clock at night three windows must be lit in every house. Anyone found out in the streets after 8 o'clock at night would be shot. Proclamations of this sort succeeded one another every day. The German authorities fairly tripped over their own regulations. They allowed the Namuriens to have their own *Bourgmestre*, but when General von Below left the town, as he did in a few days, he was succeeded by another Commander, who proceeded to unsew in regulations all that had been sewn up before. The *Bourgmestre* was in despair.

While General von Below was in the town things went well in the Convent and at our ambulance. The Germans were full of protestations and promises, and at least we obtained this exemption—we might keep the Convent doors locked at night. An order was stuck on the door giving us this permission and signed von Below. Under this, in German, was another intimation :—" Hier wohnen 174 Frauen " (Here live 174 women). I always laughed when I looked at this notice in German.

One of the Belgian wounded soldiers, who was the last to come into our ambulance, told me how the forts of Namur fell. St. Mare is a village situated about the same height as all the forts and about the centre of them. The Germans coming from Liège on one side forced a passage through the forts between Cognelées and Marchevolet and took up a position at St. Mare. Another German force coming from Dinant bombarded the southern forts and the western fort, which surrendered after two hours' attack owing to the strength of the German guns. Then the Germans attacked the Belgians and French, who had taken up a position in the plain of Belgrade, and defeated them. After this the Germans joined their northern force stationed at St. Mare, and together from St. Mare sent forces against the Belgians between the forts of Cognelées and Emines and took them in the rear, when they were expecting a frontal attack. Thus practically the position was lost. The Germans crossed the Meuse at Andenne, a small town which they burnt and where they killed 450 of the civil inhabitants, and entered Namur on the Sunday afternoon.

The last stand of the Belgians was between the forts of Emines and Suarlée. The men were left fighting there without any news of the position in the other forts or of the surrender of Namur, which had taken place on Sunday, August 23. During two days, until the morning of the 25th, they held out under the fire of the German guns, which we had heard so persistently, and then left their positions, taking a southward direction, as far as the woods of the Haute Marlagne. Here they passed the night of the 25th, were surrounded by Germans, and surrendered on the morning of the 26th. About 800 were taken prisoners near Six-Bras. The forts of Suarlée and Emines held out till the 27th and were the last to fall. Hundreds of Belgians were killed n the Plain of Belgrade during their retreat to the woods of the Haute Marlagne.

By September 3 Namur had settled down to a certain amount of calm. The German troops were perpetually going backwards and forwards through the town. Fresh regiments came up—others disappeared. They seem to have put a tidal wave of men into action, but what had they in reserve ? By September 3 all the men in Namur were Reservists, and they, thank goodness ! gave up singing. They were always wanting to have their photographs taken. A German officer came into our ambulance and said the German wounded that we had there must be taken to the military hospital. They were not really fit to go and I could see that they were very sorry to leave us. The first day they seemed to look upon us with suspicion, but they became quite friendly and said they wanted to go home. They were all men from the Rhine country. A message came through to me from one of the Red Cross ladies that about 20 English prisoners had passed through Namur station going to Germany. They were closely guarded and were not even given water to drink nor food, because, the Germans said, the English were using " dum-dum " bullets. I went and laid a complaint about this to the new German Commander of Namur. He assured me there must be some mistake, and he gave me permission to go to the station and look after any other wounded and take my nurses. We went whenever we were able and could be spared from our own Ambulance, but I did not see any more English pass through Namur, and I heard they were well treated when passing through Brussels.

When I was at the " Kommandantur " that day, there appeared to be some depression among the Germans. The head doctor of the garrison, Dr. Schilling, who had hitherto been most civil to me, seemed agitated. He looked at my passport and his hands trembled as he held it. He said, " How wicked of you English and your " Mr." Grey to fight against the Germans and leave us to those devilish Russians." I was very much struck at Dr. Schilling's room. He had his cupboard all arranged with numbers, and the receptacles were full of German envelopes with the contents plainly written upon them in blue pencil. It was in apple-pie order, and the Germans might have been in Namur for years. I used to go every day and visit the " Kommandantur " and bother the Commander and the doctor and quote the Convention of Geneva and do all I could to lighten the lot of our wounded. In spite of this the Germans soon came and took away as prisoners 30 of those who had nearly recovered.

I disliked very much trying to get favours out of the Germans, but it had to be done. They never left the Belgians one minute's peace. They annoyed them with proclamations, orders, and regulations. Nothing was permanent—for their own safety the Germans had to keep everything moving and unsettled. The people of Namur looked so utterly miserable. Dr. Schilling had a very rough manner, but I do think he had a good heart and positively hated the job in which he was engaged. He was always working to get even the badly wounded sent on as prisoners, "to evacuate," he said, "to make room for other wounded." "I must —I must," he would say angrily. I asked him if the Belgian and French prisoners were properly looked after in Germany when they were wounded. "God in Heaven! Madame," he answered, "do you take us for barbarians?"

The question of the wounded from outlying districts was becoming a very serious one. Hundreds of badly wounded French and Turcos were being brought in from the country where they had lain for nearly a week unattended in villages. Some of the Turcos' wounds were badly gangrenous. These poor African troops look so dejected and forlorn. Unfortunately one of the Belgian wounded escaped from a Red Cross Ambulance, and so I knew that Dr. Schilling had his eye on all private ambulances. He wished to get the wounded under German supervision and to close all private ambulances.

Yesterday a guard of eight German soldiers was sent into our Convent. This was really more than I could bear so I forwarded a message to the Commander and in half an hour the guard was taken away. I asked for two sentries to be left at the door. I thought this would be a good thing. These men were changed every two hours and I had long conversations with them. They all seemed anxious to go home again and knew nothing of why they were fighting or where they were going to fight. They knew they were marching to Paris—that was all. Some of them said Paris had been taken. I felt sorry for the reservists, broad faced and broad hipped. They were always talking about their wives or their work. In all their attitudes there was more depression than bitterness. One afternoon a corporal came up and told our sentries that the regiment was going away at 3 o'clock. When the sentries remonstrated that they had no orders to quit their sentry duty, he said they were to come—they had to go to Maubeuge—so they slipped off and were not replaced, and we had no more sentries in front of the Convent.

The day after the Germans took possession of Namur they gave an order that anybody who sold spirituous liquors on his premises would be shot. Only beer was sold. I never saw any cases of drunkenness in Namur.

At the station the traffic was immensely impeded, as it was necessary to get the transport through before the troops, but it was the early days of the war and the natural methodical ways of the Germans were still spick and span and effective—a well-constructed machine doesn't break down until the parts begin to give way.

Walking in the town I met one of the German wounded soldiers who had been taken out of our ambulance. He rushed up to me with tears in his eyes and thanked me for the kindness my nurses and I had shown him. He said he hoped he would not have to fight any more and would go home to Düsseldorf. A lot of his companions surrounded us and said they wished to go home, too, but almost the next day they were all sent to the front, and I expect by now are lying dead on a battlefield in France near our own brave troops. What an appalling thing is war!

At one time we were getting very hungry in Namur. An order had gone out from the Commander to revictual the town, but it was easier said than done. With the destroying of the surrounding villages and with so many troops in the town, there was hardly anything left to eat, although the nuns always managed to provide coffee and bread for the wounded. There was no milk. I had fortunately brought down some biscuits and jam from Brussels, and the nuns fed us with all they could let us have and gave us lots of fruit. We shall be ever grateful to them. The terrible dearth of news was getting on my nerves. When the Belgians met me in the street they whispered inquiries and rumours, and walked away if they thought any Germans were looking at them. Life was one long plot and counter-plot.

It struck me that it would be very difficult to get out of Belgium.

Our stretcher-bearer, Mr. Winser, was at last able to go to Brussels in a Red Cross motor. He brought back a ham, a cheese, and some marmalade. What was far more important, he fetched from the American Legation a *Weekly Dispatch* of August 30 and in this I learnt of the French reverses near Charleroi and of the English difficulties at Mons and St. Quentin.

My whole mind was now bent upon getting to Mons. Comtesse Jacqueline de Pourtalès had come back with Mr. Winser from Brussels. She said there the city was full of German wounded, but no English, and she gave a most amazing account of the marching of German troops through Brussels on August 20. The stream of men, she said, went on for 36 hours. They must have been fully prepared for months for this *coup*. The whole thing was arranged almost theatrically. She told me that Miss Angela Manners and Miss Nellie Hozier had gone down with a small ambulance of

London Hospital nurses to Mons, having got the permit from the German authorities through freely using Mr. Winston Churchill's name. The Germans like well-known people.

We heard bad news of the burning of Louvain. Some of our patients were Louvain University students and they were miserable at the burning of their University and their wonderful and world-renowned library. Some say the Germans saved the books and took them to Germany.

I wished to see the English wounded, I said, and on September 4 I obtained a permit from the Commander to visit Mons in a motor-car with a German soldier as guard. I asked for the guard, as I knew by this means our car would be able to pass everywhere in safety. Now that there were no sentries at the Convent I called all my wounded, Belgian and French, together, and told them that the time must come when they would have to go as prisoners of war to Germany; but I put them on their word of honour that none of them would try to escape from our hospital. I pointed out to them the probability that if one escaped, all the rest would be shot. One man told me that some of them had considered the idea of climbing over the Convent wall and making a dash for liberty, but they owed so much to my sisters' gentle

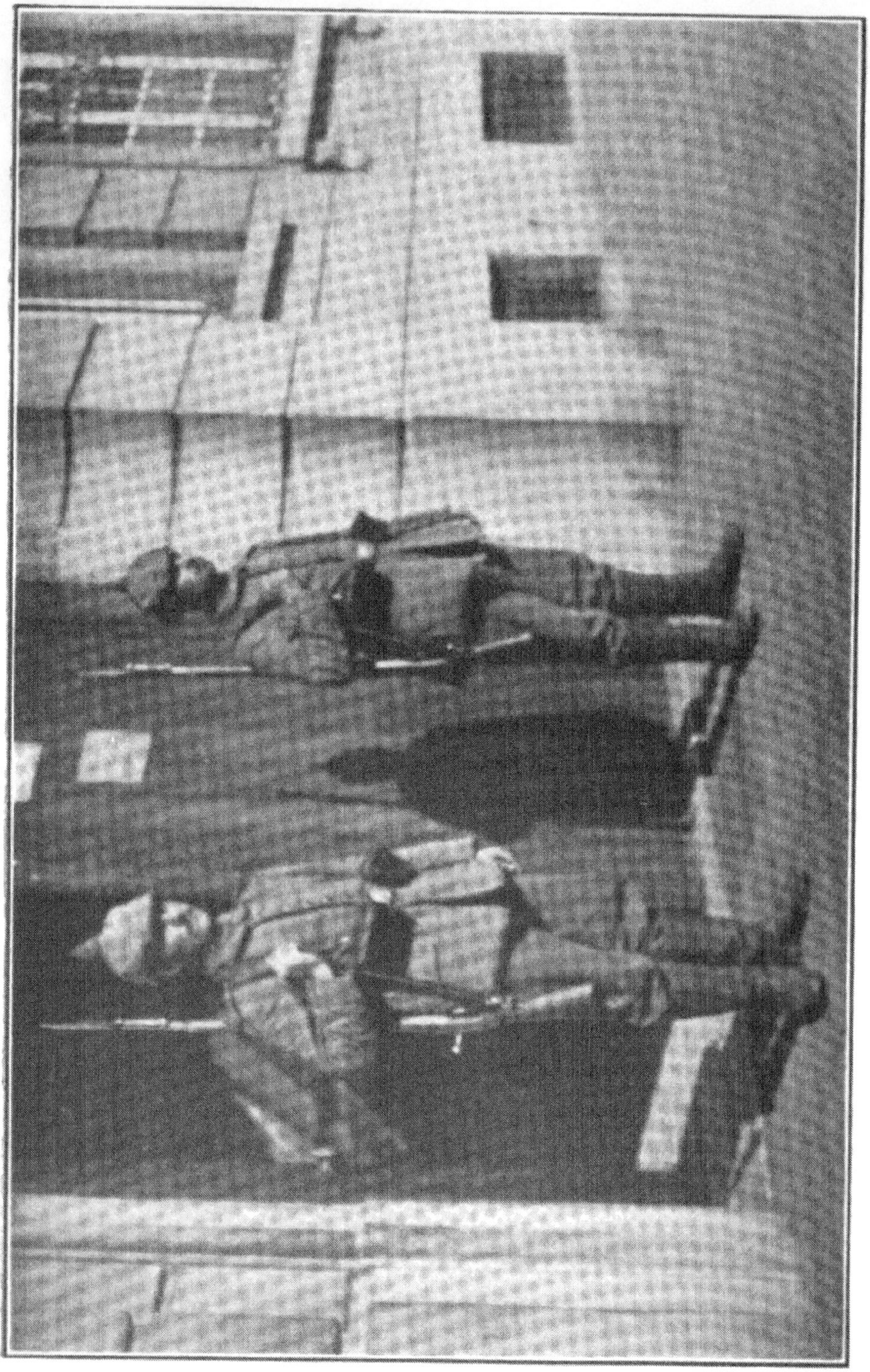

nursing and to me that they gave their word of honour they would not betray us. They kept their word too, although some of the men were quite able, if they had really tried, to elude us, and, I believe, the Germans.

CHAPTER V.

THROUGH THE GERMAN LINES IN A MILITARY TRAIN.

ON September 5, at 8 o'clock in the morning, our surgeon, Mr. Morgan, did the operation of trephining on one of our patients who had been shot in the head. As a result, he was suffering from epileptic fits. It turned out successfully. I had the pass from the Commander to go to Mons and had secured the car. The Commander asked me as a favour to take a German Engineer officer to the German lines somewhere on the frontier. We started off in gloomy silence; not even the natural gaiety of the Liégeois professor, the owner of this Red Cross car, could lighten the hour. The Engineer-Lieutenant was determined not to talk, so we determined not to talk to him. The exchange of cigarettes were the only amenities. May I hear the sound of his voice in peace days!

All the way to Charleroi from Namur along the banks of the unhappy Sambre the country was desolate. I shall never forget the burnt houses, the charred rubbish, the helpless-looking people. There had been fearful fighting in the suburbs of Charleroi. The fields were full of German graves. One grave was marked with an iron cross instead of a helmet. Soldiers walked around it each day with bare heads singing. Perhaps it was the grave of their Colonel. The persistence of the glorious weather made the contrast more tragic. Tamines was literally razed to the ground, hardly a house in the town left standing. Part of Charleroi was burnt, but I saw fewer white flags there than in Namur. In Namur from every window a white flag was hanging. In Charleroi there were German officers, and some French prisoners looking very dejected were making their way to the station.

We travelled mile after mile over the wretched "*pavées*" which make the Belgian roads so difficult for motoring. At Binche we passed through charming country and large woods. We found the Engineer's battalion at Serbe-St. Marie, a village near the French frontier. Numbers of wagons with Red Cross flags, and field transport wagons stood in the fields. Piled up by the roadside, were masses of what looked like giant coach-horn wicker baskets, I discovered they were the cases for the shells—"obus," as they call them here—used by the Feld Artillery. Between Binche and Mons the country had been freed of all troops, except the blue-coated "Landwehr" and "Landsturm," who guarded the railways and the bridges. Mons is an attractive open town with large avenues of trees. At the very first Red Cross Ambulance I found five British privates—two Royal Scots, two of the Irish Rifles, and one of the Middlesex Regiment.

The Belgian Red Cross ladies were more than kind to them but the trouble was that they could not speak English and the soldiers could not speak French. I understood from Miss Manners and Miss Hozier who had a small ambulance of London Hospital Nurses in Mons, that there were about 200 British wounded in the town, and that a whole ward of the civil hospital was full of British wounded. They were well looked after by Belgian doctors and were clean and comfortable. The heat was very great. I gathered from every man I asked that they had been surprised by the Germans on August 22 or 23. They had killed a great number but they had got separated from the remainder of the British force, and knew nothing of the sequel of the fight. "They may be all right," said one, "but, judging by the number of Germans—ten to one—I expect they were all cut up." If only we had had more English we could have killed every German."

I had to leave Mons without seeing all the English wounded. I reassured myself of the care given them. I wanted to get as near to the frontier as possible on my way back to Namur, in case of coming across any outlying wounded. The big siege cannon were still firing at Maubeuge, evidently the forts had not yet fallen. Presently we came to a country house embedded in trees with a Red Cross flag flying. I drove up and found the place belonging to Count Maxine de Bousies at Harvengt. He was nursing here 20 English wounded of the Irish Rifles, Irish Guards, Coldstream Guards, and others. Nuns were in charge, and the men assured me they were splendidly taken care of. One man was from a South Staffordshire regiment, and two men from the Wiltshire Regiment and two from the Royal Scots were in an orangery that had been turned into a hospital.

A badly-wounded patient was a young fellow belonging to the cyclists attached to a squadron of the 15th Hussars. He told me a sad story of the 15th Hussars. In the morning they had had a short skirmish with German cavalry and had beaten them off. One or two of these Germans escaped. After lunch the 15th Hussars were riding down a narrow lane when a quick-firer came round the corner with some German troops and literally blew most of them to bits—at least that was what the boy said. He declared that a shell burst under his cycle, lifted him into the air, and threw him into a wood. He was very badly wounded, but seemed to be getting on all right. I did not get his name, but he came from Gosport.

I wanted to go round by Givry, near the German guns booming against Maubeuge. The Count warned us that it would be too dangerous. What the English soldiers thought strange was that there was no answer from the forts to the German cannonading. A great desire came over me to take the motor and escape into France. But discretion proved the better part of valour, and I returned to Namur, passing on the way a quantity of German motors which were tearing along from Düsseldorf to Mons scattering German newspapers on the road as though they were having a paper-chase.

When I got back to Namur I found that the Germans had been busy; taking advantage of my absence they had announced their decision to close all private ambulances in Namur. They said they would group the wounded in two big "Lazarets" or German military hospitals. Our wounded would have to be taken to the College of the Jesuits under German control before they entrained for Germany as prisoners. I felt furious at this news, but it was too late to do anything that night as the fatal hour of 9 was passed, when all who ventured into the streets were shot. Our ambulance is such a good one; the Red Cross work in the district is well intentioned but inefficient. They were bringing from fields, villages, and isolated cottages through a wide stretch of country men who had been wounded a fortnight ago. Some were in a very bad state. Over the whole country dead and wounded were scattered like shots; frightful suffering had been entailed. I think our wounded have been lucky to have received the attention of British nurses.

In the morning I went to Dr. Schilling. He said that we could have a room at the Jesuit College in which to put all our wounded, and he gave me a note to the head German doctor at the college to this effect, but he would make no exception for our ambulance to keep it open. I was sorry for our Belgian and French wounded. They were doing so well—their dressings were often changed three times a day. They were so impressed by the gentleness of our doctor and the nurses. I think that foreign doctors, though very clever, are rougher in their treatment than ours.

'If we had no Ambulance of our own it seemed wiser to leave Namur if there were any possibility of leaving. A fearful notion came to me that we might be kept in Namur without any wounded to attend and without news. We were told there had been a battle between Alost and Ghent. Stories had reached Namur of thousands of English and Russians in the north coming to relieve Brussels. How I hoped for once that these rumours were true.

Here is a further extract from my diary, written in a German military train on September 9 :—

"Since Sunday at noon life has been a whirl. On Sunday morning I went to the Cathedral. The German Commander sat on one side of the altar and his adjutant on the other side. They were the only people beside the priests inside the altar rails. Perhaps they sought sanctuary or thought they had also taken the Almighty prisoner. After the service I went down to see the Commander. He and the German officers were at lunch at the Hotel St. Aubain. They talked in loud voices, and seemed very hungry. I sent a message in to say that I wished to speak to the Commander, and he came out from the dining-room with his aide-de-camp.

"I must apologize, Duchess," said the aide-de-camp in English, "for the growth of my beard."

I felt very indifferent about his beard, but I asked him why he did not get shaved.

"Shaved by a Belgian," he exclaimed; "why he would cut my throat!"

The Commander was delighted, he said, to help us in any way to leave Namur. I think he was getting sick of me and my ambulance. Then Dr. Schilling followed him waving his serviette and smoking a large black cigar and asked me if I had evacuated our ambulance. When I told him the Commander had said we might go to Maubeuge he called out at first, "Nein, nein," and then ran back into the dining-room. This was rather discouraging. He soon returned and said we could go when our ambulance was evacuated.

"But," I replied, "the doctor at the college declares that he does not want our wounded until to-morrow, Monday."

"Nonsense," replied Schilling, "he has nothing to do with it. They must go to-day. Even if it is Sunday I will send carts for them. When you have done what I order you, you can go to Maubeuge to-morrow."

"How are we to go to Maubeuge?" I persisted. "I have no motor."

He reflected for a moment.

"I will get you and your nurses a carriage on a German military train. You have a very good ambulance. Here is an order. You had better visit the station and see to it."

The doctor and I walked off to the station. It was crowded with troops. They had been waiting for trains to depart. The trains were hung up for days. The waiting-rooms are turned into dispensaries for the wounded as they pass through to Germany. Belgian Red Cross nurses help here.

The station master said :—" Madame, there is a train going at once with troops to Maubeuge."

I told him that I could not possibly leave until Monday and that I must have a private carriage for our nurses.

He then said :—" Please go to the doctor and tell him to ring up Liége 2 as all the carriages came from Liége, and I have not a spare one at Namur."

I went back to Schilling with the message, and left him ringing up " Liége 2," whilst I returned to my ambulance and to one of the saddest hours I have ever passed through.

They were evacuating our ambulance. It was useless for me to plead the Convention of Geneva and to prove to them by its clauses that anyone who was disabled by useless limbs for military service could be returned to their homes.

" No one is actually debarred from military service unless he is a lunatic," said the doctor.

Tears and prayers had no effect on the German authorities. All that was left for everybody was fortitude. Such fortitude as our French and Belgian wounded displayed I have rarely seen. Only "Baby-Boy," the little French chemist of nineteen, who had had his arm shattered by shrapnel, was crying.

Others, who had never even been out of bed, were sitting in chairs waiting for the cart and trying to appear as if they did not in the least mind the fearful ordeal before them. They were extremely grateful to us as the following letter to a nurse from two of the patients may help to show:—

To Sister Heron Watson.
   La Patrie et la Liberté.
   L'Union Fait la Force.

Deux étudiants de l'Université de Louvain blessés au siége de Namur et transportés à l'hopital des Anglais se font un plaisir de remercier la petite Sœur Écossaise des bons soins qu'elle ne cesse de leur prodiguer.

Ils conserveront d'elle un souvenir reconnaissant et la prient de rapporter au noble pays des Highlanders l'affectueux salut de deux soldats du petit peuple ami et allie.
        Dick and Flap.
   God Save the King!
Dieu Sauve la Patrie et puis . . . le Roi.

The nurses and I walked up the town beside the stretchers and ambulance carts that were removing them to the Jesuit College. The Jesuit brothers were very kind and very sad also. They said the Germans were taking away the wounded in a pitiable state. Some had only just been operated on, and some were in a high fever. In the big hall of the Jesuit College there were quantities of wounded all herded together. The Jesuit brothers were doing all they could for them, but, of course, it was an entirely different matter to our hospital.

When I went to say "Good-bye" to each one and wish them luck, 1 wept like a child and could not help it.

On the way back to the convent I went to see Comtesse de Pourtalès. She was now nursing in the Belgian Red Cross, at the Ecole Communale, in which all the captured Belgian military doctors, no longer allowed to wear uniform, were assisting. An order had gone out that civil doctors were not needed in the hospitals of Namur. I met the bank manager Mr. Wassage, in the street. He had been a good friend to me in Namur. He condoled with us in losing our wounded, but he was in deep grief, as his elder brother and his two sons had been taken as hostages at Dinant and shot. The boys were only twenty and eighteen years of age. There was no excuse for this except that the Germans declared some civilians had fired on them. They had razed Dinant practically to the ground, including a convent of our Namur sisters, who came afterwards for shelter to our Reverend Mother in carts.

I do not know if it is part of the tactics of war to shoot civilians wholesale as a penalty for the rashness of a few. It must be remembered that the Belgians had not had time to mobilize their army properly before the ever-ready Germans swept in, and a great many reservists, although they were not fully equipped with uniforms, &c., had arms in their houses. Many innocent lives were sacrificed for the few shots they fired, and much property destroyed. I saw no other instances of deliberate barbarity on the part of the Germans, but that was probably owing to the total prohibition of strong drink in Namur and the fact that the town had an energetic and diplomatic bishop, in whose house the German Commander lived.

The Germans were supposed to pay for everything they bought and a complaint was to be lodged if they did not do so, but, on the other hand, they raised an indemnity on Namur of a million francs to be paid immediately, and more millions to be forthcoming within six weeks.

The return to the convent was heart-breaking. All the wards were deserted. Our little helpful nuns were slopping about with pails and cleaning up; the kitten was mewing, and the old cock crowing, as he crowed quite contentedly through the bombardment, the firing, and everything else. Whilst our tears flow how happy are the animals in these days. On Monday morning there were some misleading allusions to English victories in North Belgium in *L'Ami de l'Ordre*. To us they gave a ray of hope which pierced the thick black Prussian " still-they-come " cloud ! We have to take the bitter with the sweet, for every German courtesy is wrapped round a pill of disconcerting remarks as to perpetual German victories and French, British, and Russian losses. The officers at the Kommandantur were the first to tell us of the British regiments taken prisoner and of the guns captured at St. Quentin.

In Namur Maubeuge seems to be the Mecca of the Germans. All the troops were going there, and they had either " taken it last week " or " were going to take it next week " according to the conscience of the speaker. Was this French fortress of enormous strategic importance ? I wondered. We also were to be sent to this Mecca through the desert of German occupation. I felt thankful to go to Maubeuge, for I was so tired of hearing it talked about. When I had studied the map it seemed to be only about 80 kilometres to travel. I made allowance for delay and concluded the journey ought to be accomplished in six hours.

I was soon to be disillusioned. We took our places in the train at 2 o'clock on Monday afternoon. This train, full of reservists, had been 52 hours coming from the German frontier. The train was very dirty, but the officers made room for all our nurses. They stood themselves in the corridor, which was civil of them.

One of these officers was a lawyer at home. I guessed he was a lawyer, because he told a young lieutenant to lock up the carriage next to us when he got out on the platform! He gave us some water and we offered him some cakes. He said his father had always forbidden him to eat sweet things. In spite of this he was so fat that no one could pass him in the passage. None of these officers seemed to know what was going on. This man said to me, "Have you any news of Cape Colony?" Cape Colony! when I was at that moment longing for news from England.

"You know the English have taken Togo?" he added.

"Togo—where is Togo?" I answered vaguely, hoping that it was a German frontier fortress.

"Togo—not know where Togo is!" he spluttered, and he called all the other officers to inform them of my ignorance. Of course when they said Togoland my intelligence dimly developed. But that I did not show more interest distressed them.

The German trains were irritating to me. The engines I imagined to be old, discarded goods train engines; all the rolling stock was German. One carriage was stamped "Posen," another "Altona," another "Hanover." The carriages were all decorated with lime branches and poplar branches and scribbled over in white chalk:—"To Paris"; "To Paris and London in twenty minutes"; "Come along! Antwerp has fallen."

It took this train about three hours to get to Châtelet, a suburb of Charleroi. At Châtelet I persuaded the German stationmaster to hang our carriage on to another train that was going on to Charleroi at once. We progressed for ten minutes, but owing to the congestion on the line we could not enter the station. After having been hung up for two hours on the line within sight of the platform, the doctor and I, nothing daunted by the German guards, decided to get out of the carriage and walk into the station. I have seen many fat German stationmasters, but I do not think I have ever seen such a huge man as the stationmaster at Charleroi. He ate ten eggs, and drank coffee and beer whilst he engaged us in affable conversation. He also made me write my name in his autograph book. I must say by this time we were all extremely hungry, and the more he ate the hungrier Dr. Morgan and I got. The stationmaster did not give us much hope about our train. He said it would probably go on the following morning and he was not sure if it would go to Beaumont or to Erquelinnes.

English Soldiers in a Belgian Mansion at Harvengt not far from Mons, under the care of Count Maxine de Bousies—Irish Guards, Irish Rifles, Royal Scots etc

As the station was so interesting, the doctor and I stayed some time. A long hospital train crammed with wounded passed out. The wounded were all lying on stretcher beds. There was an operating theatre on the train, also baths, and kitchens. Presently another train came in with what they called the " leicht verwundete " (slightly wounded). A number of army dressers as well as surgeons were on this train. The army dressers wear dark grey clothes with red crosses on their collars. The military doctors and dressers were always very polite to us. Some of the Germans seemed fearfully wounded, but they were going home. A few French wounded were put on this train. The stationmaster came and told us two coffins were coming out and that a guard of honour would present arms as one of the dead was a German noble and the other the son of a German minister. We stood up, and a complete hush fell upon the station as the bodies were put on the train. It was impressive and depressing.

When at last we got away from the station we found the nurses had been changed into another and much cleaner railway carriage, which had been pushed into a siding and attached to a quantity of Red Cross wagons. The other train had gone on to Beaumont with a Colonel who was in a hurry. We passed the night fairly quietly lying on the carriage seats. The day dawned cloudlessly. It seemed as if the clerk of the weather had forgotten his business. Day after day had followed each other in cloudless perfection. On September 8 it was baking midsummer heat. Our troops must have suffered. We had absolutely nothing to eat, and I felt rather sick and wretched in the early morning. The nurses were splendid. I found we had no stretcher with our equipment. A young German officer came and gave us one. Then soldiers came by drinking coffee. The German soldier cannot do without his coffee. We bought some from them. They also brought us water for washing. Presently the carriage came off the Red Cross wagons and was hung on to another troop train. I was for ever fluttering my passport to Maubeuge. We were beginning to be afraid we should have no provisions, as the soldiers said the train might not start for hours and it might go at any minute.

Two soldiers brought us two half-loaves of bread and would not accept any payment. No Belgians were allowed to come on to the railway lines. There were only troop and transport trains waiting for dispatch, and only German officials and German soldiers. They are masters of detail one must admit. Suddenly I saw two English unwounded soldiers chopping wood. We were allowed to speak to them. They were quite young boys and they both belonged to the West Yorkshire Regiment.

One came from London and one from Dublin. German soldiers were showing them how to use the chopper, to which they were entirely unused. They seemed fairly cheerful.

The German regiment in our train belonged to the 15th Infantry Brigade. They had no more news than we had, except that Maubeuge had fallen and that they were being sent down to bring back the French prisoners, 40,000 of them they boasted. We had had absolutely no news of any reliable kind. "Perhaps it is better to be lost and found than never to be lost at all," for when we are found, if the news that is sure to reach us is sad, we shall wish again for this strange oblivion.

During one of our halts a stationmaster wanted to talk to me about the war. I told him the Red Cross made a rule never to talk about the war—their occupation was to attend to the sick and wounded. But he persisted and said it was dreadful we were fighting against the Germans and were allied with the Russians. Always the Russians! I pointed out to him that whichever way the war went, "whether you win or we win," England was fighting for a righteous cause—the protection of small countries and to give the people, whether German or English, a chance of self-expression freed from military despotism.

"In spite of this, I do not see," he grumbled, "why I should be exiled here when my wife is expecting her sixth child in a month." But when he turned away a German non-commissioned officer who had been writing at the table and listening to my democratic enunciations leant forward and said in a low voice, "You are quite right, Fräulein; you are quite right."

CHAPTER VI.

THE HIDEOUS HAVOC OF WAR.

AT 3 o'clock on the afternoon of September 9 our train was still standing in the station at Charleroi. We had been there 24 hours. I decided I must somehow get food, and without anyone molesting me I forced a way through the paling near the line, which was guarded by two German soldiers, who in the heat had fallen asleep, and ran across to a café. Directly the Belgian proprietor found I was not a German he gave me a loaf of bread, refusing payment, and told me I should find mineral water at a chemist up the street. He seemed utterly dumbfounded that I was an Englishwoman travelling on a German military train. I had just returned to the train with my provisions when it started, and I saw the boy who had hurried to fetch me eggs stand disconsolately by the palings as we rolled by. At every station, Landelies, Thuin, &c., we halted for ages.

The congestion on the line must have been phenomenal. The officers on the platforms seemed surprised to see us, and asked us what we were doing; and when they heard we were "Red Cross" they gave us biscuits and chocolate.

"There is nothing else in the place," they said; "we have cleared out the eggs long ago, and the chickens are killed."

During these long halts English soldiers would have been smoking, laughing, and possibly ragging. These German soldiers got out of the train very quietly, were then marshalled together as if they were a choral union, and with a non-commissioned officer waving his arm like a baton they burst dolefully into one part-song after another. There had been a glorious sunset and now the moon was rising. This gloomy chanting seemed to me filled with the sorrow of nations. I thought of my suffering wounded now on their way to Germany as prisoners, of the dead lying on the battlefields. I had a strong suspicion that the whole scene was arranged to impress us. Surrounded by these foreign officers and their men, perfectly courteous and complacent, I felt more pitiably lonely than if I had been in the heart of a Canadian prairie.

It was a cold grey morning when we arrived at Erquelinnes a frontier town between France and Belgium.

When the train started from Charleroi I had no idea at which point near Maubeuge we should be deposited. Frontiers and Customs are of no account in the march of armies. At Erquelinnes we saw a number of transport trains carrying broken-down auto-wagons on the trucks. Indeed, these damaged transports had passed us on two trains during the night.

I do not know the exact nationality of the stationmaster at Erquelinnes. He looked quite different from the other stationmasters we had seen and was one of the most obliging men I had met in the German occupation of Belgium. He gave me a cup of hot cocoa, but this did not bias me. He really was what men call "a decent chap." He told me that he expected down from Maubeuge thousands of French prisoners. The first batch had just arrived and he was entraining "Mon Général" and his staff, I concluded the Governor of Maubeuge.

Suddenly on the platform I saw about thirty British Tommies. They were prisoners. I might speak to them if the officer allowed me to. The officer was agreeable; so I had a few minutes' chat with them. They had all been slightly wounded in or near Maubeuge and had recovered. There was only one cavalryman amongst them, Corporal Merryweather, of the 4th Dragoon Guards. There were two Cameron

Highlanders, and one man told me he came from Church Aston, near Newport in Shropshire, where I had lived. They were all fairly cheerful, and I gave them a few hints about keeping up their pluck. Of course the difficulty of understanding the English or German language for the two armies makes things most difficult for the prisoners, for if one does not understand German the sound of the language alone is unpleasant. The Englishman asked me if I would beg the German soldiers to open their ration tins as they had no knives. The German officer answered :—

"To please you, madam, it shall be done, but our men have hardly had bread to eat for three days."

The stationmaster came up and said he had got us a cart and a blind horse, and that two German soldiers should drive it for us to Maubeuge with our luggage and ambulance equipment.

"There are no motors," he said, "and the line has been blown up, so you ladies must walk."

I asked him how far it was and he said :—

"Little more than ten kilometres."

As one very nearly does that in a day's golfing, I thought it was a walk to attempt, and the nurses and doctor agreed with me. German soldiers had given my nurses coffee—a Prussian cook refused to sell it to us. I was about to give him a piece of my mind when the soldiers themselves inferred that he was a brute, so I left the matter alone. We were fairly hungry, but I had had the cocoa. My spirits had fallen to zero. It it is impossible to describe the war-swept condition of Erquelinnes. On the top of the hill on a miserable looking dwelling I saw a Red Cross flag flying. I got permission to go there with one of the usual written passes.

As we went up the deserted, rubbish-strewn street a German soldier was playing a gramophone in a ruined house. The effect was ghastly. The Red Cross flag waved on a small convent which had originally sheltered 19 nuns. Two only were left; the rest had been sent away. Five French wounded lay here, and one old woman who had been shot through the leg. The condition of the wounded was very sad. The nuns were doing their best, but no doctor had visited them for days, for they were probably prisoners. The wounded had lain for a long time on the battlefield. Legs were not set, nor wounds properly dressed. One young fellow was very much cut about with shell. The doctor took a large piece of shell out of his leg, and maggots were in the wound. He was lying with the straw that was wrapped round his leg on the field, and he screamed when he was touched. His nerves had gone to pieces. It was pitiable. I longed for an ambulance to take them to hospital. I found they had been shelling Maubeuge from Erquelinnes for over 12 days. The inhabitants had all fled long ago and the Germans had looted the town. It was on September 8 at 6 in the evening that the forts of Maubeuge had surrendered.

It was on September 10 at 6 a.m. that we arrived at Erquelinnes. That walk to Maubeuge was a memorable one. The country is a wide-stretching plain, growing corn, turnips, &c. I should guess it was a rich agricultural district. Now it was utterly deserted, save for the German troops marching up the rough, dusty roads and the French prisoners marching down them. We passed between them all, and a rushing motor-car filled with swaggering German officers occasionally cast its dust upon us. After a time we cut across country to shorten our walk, but we were perpetually tripped up by barbed wire or hindered by the deserted trenches and the huge pit-like holes which had been made by the shells. A German officer passed with a detachment of infantry. He was evidently acting schoolmaster and taking out his little lot of soldiers to explain to them how the forts had fallen. He was rude to us, but we paid no heed. Presently we struck into the French prisoners again and continued our progress between them and the German Guards. I spoke to the prisoners in French and told them that we had been nursing their wounded comrades at Namur. They then rushed forward with postcards and letters, asking us to let their relations know what had happened to them. Of course, we could only deal with a few. The Germans had told us that they had taken 40,000 prisoners. I should think that there were about 20,000, chiefly elderly reservists, " pères de famille," as they sadly told us. One man said, "We could have held on days and days in the forts, only they gave us the order to surrender." The German Guards called out to us good-humouredly :—

" What are you ? "

" International," I replied, " for the sick and wounded."

" Ach, nein ! Engländerin " (No ! Englishwoman !), they said, laughing amongst themselves.

They seemed much interested in us. Presently we came to a village. Every house was either ruined or deserted. In some houses the food was still on the table and the washing in the tub. What a frantic departure the inhabitants must have made ; all around this village we saw dead cattle and horses swollen and stiff, killed by shell fire. There was a dreadful smell. I saw no human dead bodies, but numbers and numbers of long mounds, which were graves marked by empty shells and German helmets stuck on the top. Here and there were a few crosses. It was all heart-breaking, but still we walked, until we actually came to a farm that had not been destroyed. The owner sold us some eggs and gave us some coffee. She was a garrulous lady, and told us how she had got the right side of the Germans, and all her homeless neighbours sat round her piteously wondering why they had not been able to do so also. I christened that farm " La maison des mouches," the " house of flies." I had never seen so many flies in a house before. We went away with our eggs in an empty lyddite shell, and when we got to the next village we found the German soldiers had changed the blind horse and commandeered another horse, which promptly ran away, broke the traces, and upset the cart and all our luggage into the middle of the road. It took half an hour to quell that horse and get a new cart, but I must admit that the German soldiers did this, and on we went again. I took a photograph of a house which had been destroyed by shell fire. The whole front was blown away, only the bed stood unconcernedly in an upper room amid the débris.

When we had walked to within three miles of Maubeuge we met two squadrons of French Chasseurs. They were still riding their own horses, but they looked pretty miserable under a German escort. Then came a battery of field artillery. The officer asked me the way.

I did not know it. How I hated that devilish German artillery; one never seemed able to escape from it—the fat black howitzers, like over-fed slugs, and the larger cannon, covered with wreaths and mottoes and their mouths protected by leather caps in the intervals of their hideous shouting. It was perfectly impossible to find out the history of the fall of Maubeuge with so many Germans about, but I did hear that the 17-inch siege cannon had been there for a long time, sunk in the backyard of a German gentleman's house who lived in the vicinity, and that they had been brought there as coal. The story sounds improbable.

The dreariest part of the day was meeting the poor people on the roads. They were going back with small bundles on their backs to their homes.

"Ma maison est-elle brulée, madame ?" they would ask, and what *could* one reply as they passed on ?

The Germans have a habit when they have conquered a place, burnt it partly and terrified it wholly, of plastering it with proclamations and surrounding it with guards and then saying, or rather coaxing, "Now go and be happy, my children, all is well; you have my permission, under certain stringent conditions of course, to fish in the rivers." I used to see frightened-looking individuals stealing forth to the banks of the

Sombre or the Meuse, as the case might be, with fishing rods before I left Namur—strong is the ruling passion even in war.

It was quite late in the evening when we reached Maubeuge. We had passed two forts on the way flying the German flag. These forts, however, only looked like raised hillocks of a peculiar construction. Buried in trees, the small town of Maubeuge is picturesque. A moat that surrounds it, the stone wall, and the fine gateway by which we entered over the bridge were intact, but in the streets war had played havoc. The only inn open had had many of its windows smashed by a shell which destroyed a great portion of the Red Cross Hospital opposite. It was evident that the Germans had deliberately shelled the town, and that may have been the reason why the forts were told to surrender. On September 11 there was no fighting round Maubeuge and no trace of the Allied Armies. They must have gone far into France. I remember hearing at Mons of the admiration of some German officers at the way in which our small English force had retired—"replié" was the word used. They said openly in the café within hearing of a Belgian gentleman who could understand German, that they had expected to take the whole force prisoners and thought the English had done a masterly stroke.

I determined, as Maubeuge was invested by the Germans, to report myself to the Commander, Major Abercron, at Headquarters. He asked me to bring in all the nurses and the doctor to his private room, and informed me that the French Red Cross were giving him a lot of trouble, that he had shot a doctor and even a nurse for being spies, and as he did not like to see a "high-born lady in an invidious position" he thought that we had better leave Maubeuge as soon as possible, or rather he regretted that he could not avail himself of our services!

He asked, "What, under the circumstances, do you wish to do?"

It was the first critical moment of difficulty that I had had so far with the German authorities. I had to call all my Scottish mother-wit to my aid.

"Our only object, mein Herr, is to nurse the wounded. Perhaps you will allow us to proceed into France, where we might find our own troops."

This amazing request on my part caused him to reflect. He was now joined by Baron W——, whose name I will not give as he had evidently known me before the war.

"You cannot go into France," said Abercron. "Have you any money on you?"

"I have sufficient," I replied.

"Then I will give you a pass," he said, "to enable you to go to England. If it is necessary to pay for services required you will do so."

I said, "I will try to go to Boulogne."

"No," he said, "not Boulogne. Boulogne is invested by the Germans. Baron W—— will get you an omnibus belonging to the hospital here. You must return it in three days. You will be accompanied by two members of the French Red Cross, who are accustomed to driving this motor, and I advise you to make your way to Ostend; you must give me your word of honour that if you fall in with British troops you will get out of the motor and not allow your English to capture it."

British troops. The very idea of them made me thrill. I had a vision of wrangling with Field-Marshal Sir John French on a Belgian roadside over my word of honour and this motor-car! I agreed, of course, to all the German's proposals. The position was difficult, and at all costs we must get away. The night we were forced to spend in the pothouse in Maubeuge was a very unpleasant one. The German officers objected to our having any rooms, and a German civilian doctor who had just arrived in the town was offensive in fluent English.

I said, "If you wish to abuse nine ladies, Sir, pray do so in German. It sounds better."

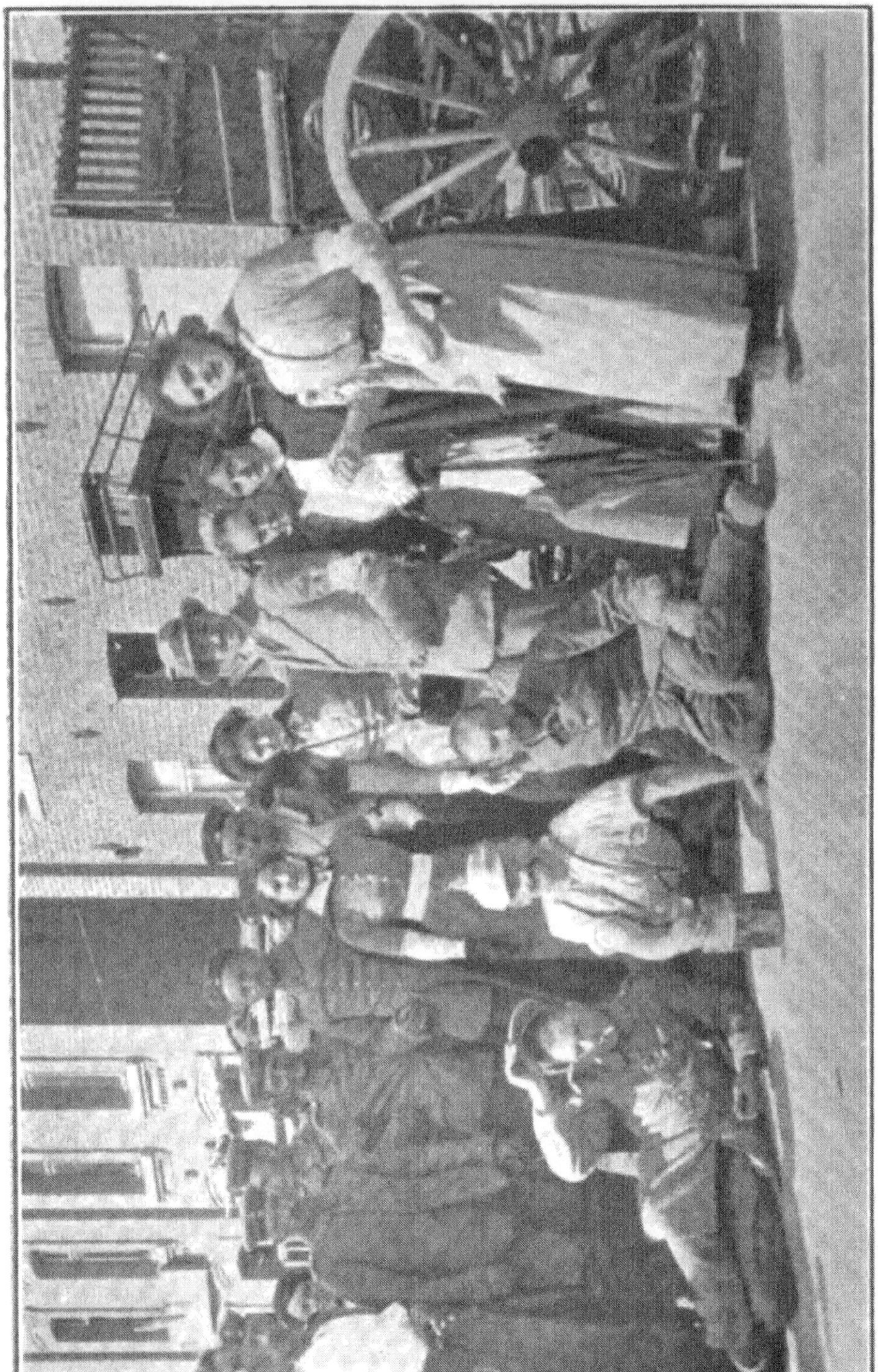

We got rooms at last, and I was fortunate in having one in which the windows had all been smashed by a shell, so there was plenty of air. One of the nurses slept on a mattress beside me. In the other room the nurses made ropes of towels and hung them over the window ledge in case of emergency! The doctor, with true British calm, sat in the courtyard writing his diary until a half-drunken German officer came and shook his fist at him, and said that if he did not go to the kitchen he would have his face off him. The doctor went to the kitchen. It is annoying how well a large number of the German officers speak French, and even English. I cannot help being ashamed of the fact that a large portion of our most intelligent and active soldiers and sailors do not speak any foreign language at all.

The omnibus appeared at 6 o'clock in the morning, and we left Maubeuge without any further restrictions, my only regret being that owing to exhaustion and the difficulty of the position I did not venture to visit the Red Cross hospitals which were full of French wounded. I left them a large quantity of our ambulance dressings, which unfortunately we had no room to take with us. We were soon bowling along a fine French road in the direction of Bavai. It was much cooler and rain was beginning to fall. We saw hardly any Germans on this road and the villages were not destroyed. All the people rushed out as we passed. I think they imagined we were German nurses, which was tiresome. At Bavai I asked in the Red Cross hospitals if there were any English, but they said they had all gone away as prisoners. We then went on to Valenciennes. Here the people crowded round our car. I had stopped to buy some food. They called out, "Has Maubeuge fallen ? Has Maubeuge fallen ?" They looked very miserable when I told them the news. A doctor came up and reported three English soldiers in the Valenciennes Hospital. I found Captain George Belville, of the 16th Lancers, there and two men of the South Lancashires. It was a good hospital and they were all doing well. Captain Belville had been shot in the right arm by a French soldier who had taken him for a German as he was stooping down to help a man on the ground. At a distance of about 400 yards German and English might easily be taken for each other. Of course, at close quarters they are totally unlike.

The first line of the German Army is impressive, brave, I should say, and fierce, and conveyed all the moral effect to Belgium that the Germans intended. After the first line the physique of the men is inferior. They seem to have no heart for the war, and would always be coming up to me to speak of their wives, their homes, and their work. They respected the Red Cross in those early days. They said they would far rather work than fight, but that Germany was winning so easily the war would not take long. They did not know why they were fighting, and brought forward most ridiculous reasons. I think they were told as many lies as possible to keep up their hopes.

Only a very few German troops were in Valenciennes on September 11. Except for the guards on the bridges one would have doubted German occupation. At Valenciennes I hesitated which road to take. My passport had been very successful so far, and my great desire was to go on to Lille, find the road to Boulogne, and chance it. Why did they say Boulogne was in the hands of the Germans? When we reached Tournai, which I visited to see if there were any English wounded, a priest whom I met on the road, and to whom I gave some of the post-cards which the French prisoners had begged us to get through to their relations, told me that they had just received notice of the passage of 40,000 German troops through Lille that day. This seemed a formidable number to encounter, so I made my greatest tactical mistake and turned north into Belgium, hoping to reach Ostend. A rumour had filtered through to Tournai that a number of English and Russian troops were in the north of Belgium and in possession of Antwerp, Ghent, and Malines. Once in Belgium, however, the German Guards on the roads began to get more frequent. We got past three patrols of Uhlans in safety. I used to stop the car 20 yards away from them and walk to meet them, holding out my passport. The third patrol searched my apron pockets for arms and then searched the motor till I began to wish that I had taken the French road. At Renaix we came to a full stop. We had run into a base of the German Army. A young officer got on to the car and took us to the Headquarters of the Staff at the inn. I told him that I was on my way to Ostend by Oudenarde and Bruges. He repeated this to the Brigadier who was having luncheon with his officers, and my desire was greeted with a shout of laughter. I thought I had better go in and confront them all whilst they were eating and drinking. The Brigadier was perfectly civil.

"Die Frau Herzogin" was quite right—the shortest way to Ostend was by Oudenarde and Bruges—Abercron was a very good fellow—but how could he tell at Maubeuge the impossibility for an ambulance to pass from their lines into the British lines! No, no. I must go back to Brussels—no distance—only 30 miles, and get my commands from Feld-Marschal von der Goltz, Governor of Belgium, &c., and to make the way easy some officers would go in a motor before us and show us the way.

For the first time I felt powerless. Brussels was the one place I did not wish to return to. I knew how difficult it would be to get out of that city and how expensive to stay there. On many occasions obedience is a virtue ; this was one of them. The Frenchmen with us, who had been rather enjoying the outing, grew pale. It was not my fault that the motor could not be returned to Maubeuge in three days, but that of Abercron's compatriots ; so I washed my hands of all further responsibility. As I stepped back into the motor a German private suddenly ran out of the ranks and wrung my hand.

"Madame, Madame," he cried sympathetically, to the utter amazement of his comrades.

I have wondered since if he could have been a London waiter. At break-neck speed, swaying dangerously behind the German car, we followed on, once more returning to the centre of German occupation.

CHAPTER VII.

OUT OF GERMANY'S CLUTCHES.

WE were back in Brussels at 4 o'clock. Alas! how different to the bright confident city I had left a month ago. Everyone knows the charm of Brussels. For the moment it seemed to have slipped this charm into dark shadows to watch for a new day dawn. The Germans had not taken away all the Belgian flags. I hear the Bourgmestre had protested, so I saw a few hopefully waving, but there was no doubt of the German possession In the streets were their soldiers and sailors, their tinkers. and their tailors, and the supernumerary army of private detectives and spies that form the German advance guard. Where was the French Red Cross Hospital at Le Cercle Artistique? Alas! the French Red Cross sisters were hidden away—no hospital—the Cercle remained a club for German officers. A great many of the private ambulances had been suppressed.

The Palace was full of German wounded. Baron Lambert's hospital, which he had lavishly equipped, was practically empty. There were, of course, few French and no English wounded in Brussels, but every day fresh consignments of German wounded came in and were driven by side streets in the dusk of the evening to the "lazarets," as they call them. The Germans hate the Belgians to see them bring in their wounded.

Poor Brussels! The good days will come again for her; now she weeps, pretending to the Germans that her tears are smiles, so much pluck has she. The officers waved to us to follow them, and up the hill we went to a "Kommandantur" once again. Von der Goltz was out—"watching a battle, as usual, I suppose," remarked a Yankee. The officers gave us specious assurances of his speedy return, and advised that we should go to the Hotel Astoria to eat and rest, but as the motor turned the corner of the street two German guards jumped on to it and I began to see we were in for some fun. I took the precaution of removing my baggage from the car, and at the moment nothing seemed to matter but the fact that I had a bedroom with a bath attached to it, and that it was possible to have poached eggs and buttered toast! With such privileges how could I distress myself when the manager came to tell me in frightened tones that I was a "prisonnière" and that the Germans had actually placed two sentries at my bedroom door. My conscience was clear in regard to those ostentatious Teutons, their "moral effect" had been so small on my imagination, that I felt sleep to be all I needed, sleep where I might dream of peace, of green English fields, of some joyous reassurance that I should never have to see a German again. When the nurses came in the morning there seemed no interference with their movements—but when they told me that the sentries were still there and that a private detective had taken the doctor away I knew that something must be devised.

The previous evening I had seen a Belgian representative from the American Legation. I now felt that at all costs I must see the American Minister himself. I managed to get a note through to him. He most kindly came, but at my door the sentries refused to let him in. He told me afterwards that he went to the Kommandantur and " raised ——!" The result was very successful. An officer came round with him, cursed the sentries—as if it was their fault—and they were removed. The American Minister, Mr. Brand Whitlock, is a very agreeable man. He had been appointed by President Wilson as Minister to Brussels for a rest cure! He has been for some years con-

ix.   House destroyed by shell on route to Maubeuge.

ducting a semi-Socialist campaign against crime on his own lines, and with success I was told, as Mayor of Toledo, U.S.A., and has written several books. Unfortunately for him destiny had checkmated his rest cure, but I am quite sure that this man of peace was in a great many ways checkmating the Germans. I owe him gratitude, not only for the pleasure of his acquaintance, but for his efforts on behalf of my ambulance.

His visit was succeeded by that of Count H—— von H——, working in the German Red Cross, who, as being an old friend, was sent round to identify me! He asked me as a favour if I had heard in my wanderings of a Prince who was supposed to be badly wounded near Mons. So the Germans have their "missing," too! My anxiety was chiefly about the doctor, who I feared might be spirited away to Germany without my being able to assist him. After two hours he returned and gave a cheerful account of how he had been searched. His chief great joy was that he had managed to save his diary. H—— von H——assured me that I was as free as the air, and that though the Ostend route was barred I might take the next train to Holland. So much for the American influence! Of course, there was no "next train," but we still had the Maubeuge motor, and it became more and more important that as we could not nurse in Brussels or get to Antwerp that we should leave Belgium. Therefore, I presented my compliments to Major-General von Lüttwitz, Military Governor of Brussels, and asked him how soon we could go to Holland in the motor. General von Lüttwitz presented his compliments to me in return and said he would call on me at the hotel. On receiving this news I rose and dressed, and, surrounded by all my nurses, received him in the salon. He was affable, and said we could have the motor and travel by Liège and Aix-la-Chapelle—commonly called Aachen—to Holland.

"But not with the Frenchmen, they had seen too much; they would work in the Brussels hospitals."

"I do not want to go by Aachen," I said—well I knew Aachen was in Germany. "I wish to go a shorter road which I know of to Maastricht."

"I also know the shorter road," he said, "but as you ladies are——" he hesitated—"our guests, I must see to your safety. By the short road the Belgians are treacherous. They might shoot the Germans who will be driving your car. I cannot allow that. They are very restless in the north."

I began to note that the "moral effect" of the German invasion with all its fearful pomp was beginning to wear off the Belgians.

"Very well," I replied, submissively.

It was no use arguing. I had a feeling that this General respected the English. He had been attached to our forces during the Boer War. When he had gone, I went round to the American Legation and had lunch with Mr. and Mrs. Whitlock. I told Mr. Whitlock that when he sent me roses the girl who brought them said :

"We never sell flowers for ladies now. We only make wreaths for the German princes and nobles who die in the hospitals."

Although I had accepted a German passport to reach Holland by Aachen and agreed to start on the morning of September 15, I was quite determined to search for all possible means to avoid going that way. To get into Germany might mean not getting out again.

"What about Jim Barnes going with you?" said the American Minister.

"Jim Barnes," as I discovered, was an American writer and traveller, and as he had to carry dispatches to The Hague he seemed the very man for us. Besides he loved an adventure, and to escort an English ambulance in safety out of German administration was an adventure all to itself. He readily agreed to come with us, and by this means he prevented a German officer from occupying the front seat. He sat between the two German soldiers, a fine burly protector, and the German officer was left behind. The Stars and Stripes seemed to flap in Brussels a little uncomfortably in the eyes of the Prussian dictators.

Our motor was now fairly loaded and I shall always wonder why it did not break down, for the Germans did not understand its mechanism as well as the Frenchmen. When I suggested calling at the Red Cross Hospital at Namur to see the Comtesse de Pourtalès and Mr. Winser, who had remained with her, the German lieutenant called out, "Nein, nein, kein Besuch!" (No, no—no visiting), which I considered extremely officious on his part. However, as I was anxious to press on to Liége, Namur had to be neglected. My blissful ignorance of war events had been dispelled. I knew again good from evil. I had seen some back numbers of *The Times*— our casualty lists and Sir John French's account of the Glorious Retreat. Binding this knowledge on to my own experiences I pictured the whole situation and felt miserable. Yet behind the misery sprang a great hope and belief as to the ultimate outcome of things which could not now be shaken by heartaches or personal loss.

A number of Belgians collected round the motor and I saw some of my old friends belonging to the Red Cross. A sad farewell to them indeed. I assured them we were not prisoners and begged them to come and see me in

England. There was a suspicion in my mind that the terror of the Belgians under German rule was passing—that after all she had suffered and was suffering Belgium was regathering her forces, and my prayers went out for her.

My last experience in Brussels was the salute of a German soldier. He had brought me a receipt from the General signed by our two Frenchmen, for some money I had sent them through him. May Prussia realize in time, as Freiherr von Lüttwitz realized, that honesty is ever the best policy !

It was only when we reached the outskirts of Brussels and assured our motor-driver that he was taking the wrong road to Namur that we noticed that a small car was preceding us. It was driven by a German lieutenant, and in it were evidently two German private detectives. Our car had been told to follow it—there was no question about that ; we drove round and round the Forêt de Soignes till we found the right road. So much for the German bump of locality. We passed a large number of "Landwehr" and "Landsturm" troops on the march. These are small and sturdy men, but they marched wearily. I was told they were from Alsace and Lorraine. The day before I had heard of fresh troops passing through Namur with artillery going north ; they had been hurried up from the Rhine

Provinces because the Belgians had blown up the line between Louvain and Liège, and the rumour had become more persistent of strong Russian and British reinforcements in the north.

It was one of the most effective rumours I had so far come across. The Germans were concerned. The night before I left Brussels there had been quite a panic in the hotel. The Belgians had killed some German marines and bluejackets near Louvain; the Germans had been surprised without efficient artillery, and at first the German officers in Brussels believed the affair to be something of far larger magnitude. I was told they packed up all their things and went post haste to the station, but on learning the truth returned to the hotel. Certainly the Germans in Brussels were in a " jumpy " state at that time. The detective car went with us all the way to Namur, kept breaking down and catching us up again. I am at a loss to know why those gentlemen were put to so much trouble. Outside Namur it watched us into the town and left us.

Once more we were in Namur. The photographer's was closed, the doctor could not get his films. We saw a nun opening the convent door, but before she had time to recognize us we had sped past. Namur seemed very quiet. We were now on the road to Huy, passing through Andenne. It was not so badly destroyed as I had been led to believe; only half the town was burnt. The Germans were busy putting up temporary wooden bridges. The Belgians had blown up many bridges over the Meuse in their endeavour to stop the German advance. I had never been through the valley of the Meuse before; I was struck with its beauty. How peaceful and happy the inhabitants must have been before this dreadful war. It was hateful to see wrecked houses and homeless people amid so much of nature's fairness. Liège is a big city, full of ironworks and long stretching suburbs, and I quite understood how much better it had held out than the small town of Namur. The people of Liège are very much alive. Presently they may give their temporary conquerors some trouble. On the railway at Liège there was a great congestion of transport and troop trains. The direct line from Liège to Brussels was, owing to the tactics of the Belgians, unavailable. German troops were bivouacking around the trains and looked as if they had been waiting days for departure. Liège held a German Headquarter Staff and was full of hospitals. I saw German nurses walking about here. A doctor wanted to commandeer our motor.

"We are getting short of motors," he said, "to bring in our wounded."

This remark struck me as very strange, as we had seen a perfect array of motors in the town. I confess the situation for Englishwomen in Liège was not promising. I am quite sure that if Mr. Jim Barnes, U.S.A., had not had us under his protection we might have had unpleasant experiences of a kind which we had hitherto been almost spared.

Two rather pathetic incidents, however, in relation to the English came to my notice.

A German baron who knew my sister said he had been called back to be a soldier after twelve happy years in England. "I have left all I love there," he said.

Another young lieutenant on the German General Staff at Liège told Mr. Barnes he was engaged to an English girl. Mr. Barnes offered to take a note to her. "What would be the use of writing to her," replied the lieutenant sadly. "Can she still care now?"

Mr. Barnes succeeded in getting us passports to go through to Holland by Canne, and Aachen was left out of the programme! We never showed our original passports from Brussels to the Liège Commander, for very naturally he had exclaimed that to go to Aachen was a very long way out of our road. We spent the night at the Hotel de l'Europe as Americans, and left next morning in bright sunshine. We had only an hour and a half before us.

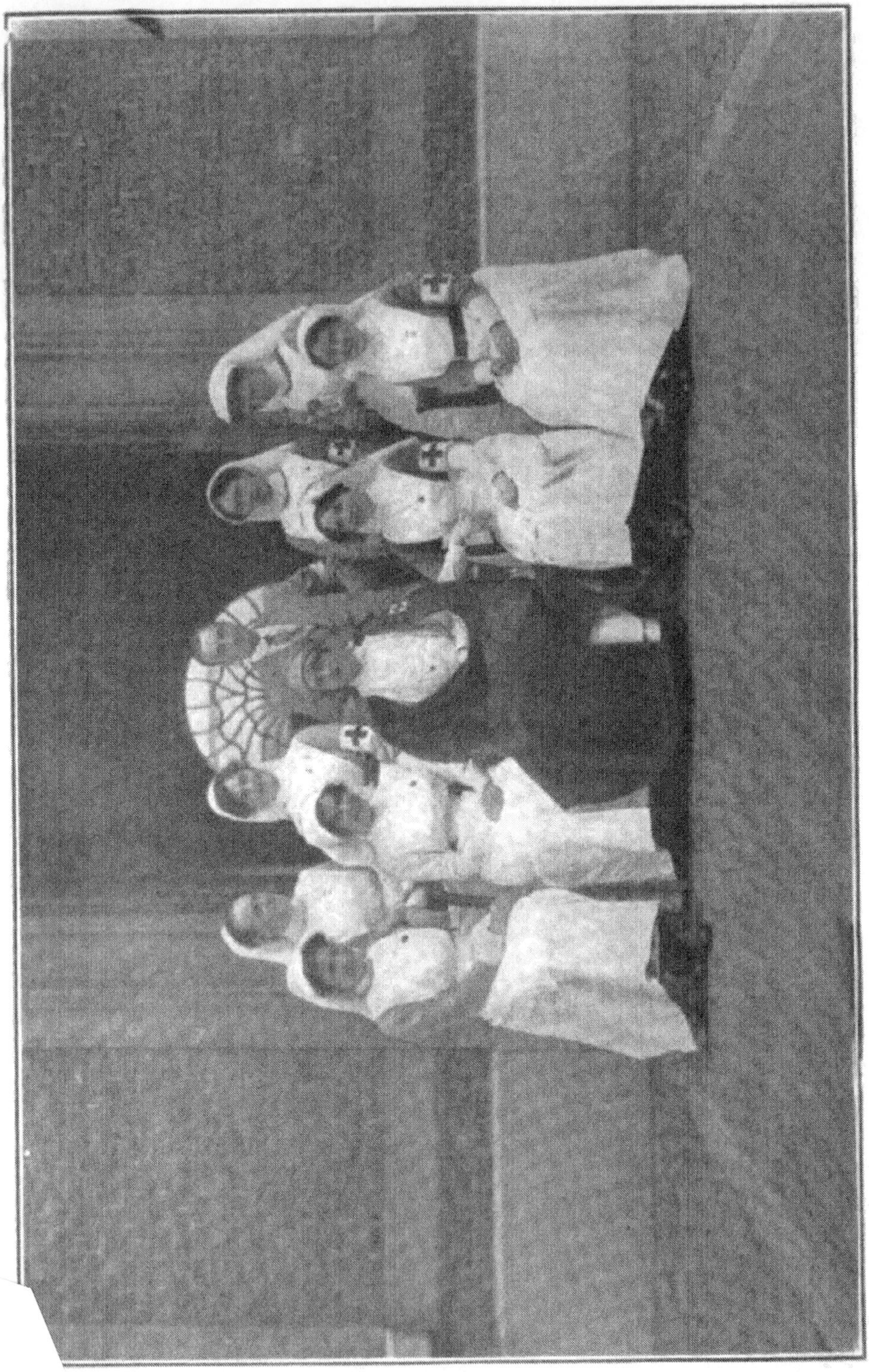

I seemed to count the minutes till we left Liège. I was so homesick that it was difficult to keep up my spirits and not betray that we were depressed by the last few days of inaction and stupendous difficulty. My nurses were marvellous, accepting all events with perfect equanimity and showing an unflagging interest in everything that happened.

"We are nearly in Holland," I exclaimed at last.

"Oh!" said one of them, "I hoped it might be France. We do want to go on nursing."

But when we jumped over the little row of Dutch flags in the middle of the road at Canne and found ourselves in a friendly company of Dutch infantry, who gave us seats in an orchard and fed us with green apples, I knew how wonderful it was to be in a land of peace again. The last two places we passed before reaching the Dutch frontier were the saddest of all—Visé and the village of Eben-Esael. In the last-named village every house had been burnt. Carriages came out to Canne to fetch us into Maastricht, three miles away. Mr. Barnes had ordered these. He was a splendid organizer. The motor sped away on its return with the German drivers; they had been handsomely tipped, but I had the malicious satisfaction of knowing that Germany had paid for all the petrol we used from Maubeuge to Maastricht!

Maastricht was full of Belgians eager to learn our experiences, eager to know all that we had been going through, and what was happening in their dear country. It is a strange town just now, for every nationality is harboured here. I should think the tales that could be gathered at Maastricht of hairbreadth escapes and thrilling experiences would make the plots of many novels and plays. We left Maastricht in the evening *via* Utrecht for The Hague. Once more we were buying tickets and travelling on ordinary passenger trains. Only those who have seen the deadly swift changes wrought by war can comprehend how six weeks could feel exactly like six years. When we reached The Hague I was utterly worn out. A telegram brought me private good news which revived me. Odd enough it was to get a telegram again. In Brussels there was nothing but the German Feld-Post, no newspapers were allowed to be published; someone who brought me a back number of *The Times* had to button it inside his waistcoat.

I wished we had been able to bring away the English Red Cross contingent left in Brussels. A few of them were nursing Germans. Some were allowed in the station to tend wounded prisoners as they passed through, but the difficulty of getting away from Brussels was almost phenomenal, and had it not been for the Maubeuge motor I believe we should still have been there ourselves. The troubles in Brussels for the English must have very much increased. Doctor Wyatt and Mr. Tweedie, who came to see me, told me every now and then one or two of them would be taken away and searched. Of course they could no longer wear khaki. I brought many letters and messages from them to the Red Cross offices in London, and I hope money has now been sent them.

Holland was mobilized for war, of course. All the bridges were stacked with explosives ready for sudden emergencies, the stations were guarded by troops. But still all was peace; the homesteads smiling, the cattle grazing comfortably, young men playing football, nothing burnt, nothing destroyed! Holland opened her arms with a kiss of welcome to all who cried for her protection. The contrast indeed of Peace and War! Heaven keep Holland in Peace.

The Hague is a miniature city of delight; like an ancient English print in a faded frame. I asked Sir Alan Johnston, the British Minister, to take me to the Palace of Peace. It was late in the evening and the gates were closed. I am afraid this modern building is so ugly that it will offend the rumoured artistic tendencies of the German Emperor when he does penance there! The hotel was full of Americans and of Belgians, and some gentlemen wandered around who called themselves "independent reporters." I should be inclined to call them independent informers. The spy fever rages on the Continent. I could not have passed through it untainted; I reached England and talked about spies, and I was told I was overstrung! None the less, when the history of the war comes to be written the part that systematic espionage has played for years in the fate of nations should earn its own romantic record. I have come to the conclusion that there is nothing that cannot happen—that nothing in fact is unbelievable in this world. On September 18, after all the members of "The Millicent Sutherland Ambulance" had been photographed at 6 in the morning by Mr. William Sutherland, a Dutch gentleman who bore the old name, and who presented me with a beautiful bouquet of flowers tied with the Dutch colours, we left for Flushing, *via* Rotterdam. For the first time I passed down the Channel behind outposts of British submarines and torpedo destroyers to England and home.

NOTE.

"The Millicent Sutherland Ambulance" could never have been established or have successfully done its few weeks' work in Belgium without my friends' support. I append a list of their names:—

E. J. Wythes, Esq.
Col. E. Vickers
Mrs. Hamilton-Evans
Mrs. Walker Munro
Sir Evelyn De La Rue
W. Lockett Agnew, Esq.
Lady Victoria Manners
William Harrison, Esq.
F. Shaw, Esq.
Lt.-Col. Percy
Mrs. Calverley
Miss Hudson
Miss Maxine Elliott
Lady Forbes-Robertson
Alexander Bruce, Esq.
Mrs. Paul Singer
Frederick Behrens, Esq.
Alfred C. Hunter, Esq.
Mrs. Hunter
R. A. Knowles, Esq.
Mrs. Mitchell
Miss Mitchell
Henry Hudson, Esq.
Mr. Calverley
Rev. and Mrs. Lewis Gilbertson
Mrs. Howson
Mrs. Weaver
Roscoe Brunner, Esq.
Mrs. Barrow
F. Chesterton, Esq.
Gordon Leith, Esq.
Mrs. Husband
Mrs. George Coats
Sir Thos. Glen Coats, Bart.
Dr. Russell
Earl Curzon of Kedleston
Thos. Twyford, Esq. (collected in N. Staffordshire)
W. Lovell, Esq.
Miss Mildmay
Sir Charles Morrison-Bell, Bart.

- The Staff Windsor Hotel, Glasgow
- Lord Cecil Manners
- Mrs. Frank Reynolds
- Miss Azeline Lewis
- Lady Ratcliffe Ellis
- Mr. Winser
- Mr. Cundall
- Mrs. Heber Percy
- Mrs. Henry Capel-Cure
- Mrs. Charles Hunter
- Sir William Lever
- Mrs. Carnegie
- J. Buchanan, Esq.
- Miss Monroe
- H. E. Monroe, Esq.
- B. Inglis-Marriott, Esq.
- Miss Millicent Phelps
- Mrs. Lilian Kirkness
- Mrs. Stephen Williamson
- Anonymous
- Sir Reginald Macleod, C.B.
- — Prout, Esq.
- Major Shute
- Brigadier-General Hickie

and others

In a short time I shall be returning to the Front, in connexion with the Red Cross; this time I sincerely trust among our own troops. To help them as far as possible in their fearful ordeal I shall take a fully-equipped motor ambulance, surgeons, and nurses, and all the experience I have gained in these strange days.

Further help to my Fund will be gratefully acknowledged.

TRANSLATION OF PASSPORT.

The Duchess of Sutherland has permission to go with her doctor and eight sisters from Namur to Maubeuge. May be allowed to pass everywhere, and may travel on military trains.

THE COMMANDER OF NAMUR.

The Pass of the Commandant of Namur to enable the Duchess to go to Maubeuge.

xii   The Passport of the Governor of Maubeuge allowing the Duchess to return to England.

TRANSLATION OF PASSPORT.

The Duchess of Sutherland is allowed with her doctor—Dr. Morgan—and eight sisters to travel to England. All facilities are to be given her to accomplish this, and payment may be asked.

THE GOVERNOR OF MAUBEUGE.

GAZETTEER OF TOWNS MENTIONED.

AIX-LA-CHAPELLE.—Known in German as **AACHEN**. A town and watering place of Western Prussia, situated between the Meuse and the Rhine in the Rhine province, forty-four miles west south-west from Cologne, on the line of railway from Cologne to Liége. Although situated in German territory, Aix is practically the point of junction of the German, Belgian, and Dutch frontiers, and is a town of considerable importance, with a population of nearly 150,000. Its thermal baths are widely celebrated, and it is one of the great Customs stations of Western Germany. Two treaties of peace have been signed here—the first in 1668, the second in 1748.

ANTWERP.—Capital of the Belgian province of the same name, situated about fifty miles from the sea and twenty-five miles north of Brussels by rail, on the right bank of the River Scheldt. It is one of the chief European ports, over sixty shipping lines having their headquarters here, and the quay accommodation extends nearly three miles along the bank of the river. The total population is about 400,000. Antwerp is surrounded by a ring of forts of modern design, the strongest line being that toward the east and south, where eight forts, placed at regular intervals, less than a mile distant from each other, defend the city. In addition to the regular ring of defences, the forts de Wavre and de Waelhem, in the south-east, and Fort de Schooten, in the north-east, form outpost defences. On the west forts St. Marie, St. Philippe, de Zwyndrecht, and de Cruybeke, defend the approaches to the Scheldt, which has to be crossed before the city can be reached from this direction. The Government was transferred from Brussels to Antwerp on August 17.

BRUSSELS.—Capital of Belgium and of the province of Brabant situated near the middle of the country, on the Senne, some 27 miles by railway from Antwerp. It has a population of about 700,000, and is the greatest centre of Belgian industry. It is still celebrated for its lace; considered the best in the world. The making of " Brussels carpets " is, however, not an industry of the city. It has numerous institutions of public instruction, including the free University (founded in 1834). The Royal Library contains nearly half a million volumes. Brussels was taken by the French in 1701, by the Duke of Marlborough in 1706, by the French in 1746, and again in 1792. Between 1815 and 1830 it was the capital, alternately with The Hague, of the Netherlands, and in 1830 became the capital of the new kingdom of Belgium. In 1910 an international exhibition was opened by King Albert; on August 15 the British Section, which covered 21,000 metres, was destroyed by fire. The other sections were practically untouched. The loss was estimated at £2,000,000 and included priceless exhibits lent by the South Kensington Museum.

Brussels was occupied by the Germans on August 20. Preparations were made to transfer the Government to Antwerp on August 17.

CHARLEROI.—A town of nearly 28,000 inhabitants, and the centre of the iron industry of Southern Belgium. It was fortified up to 1868, when its fortifications were converted into promenades. It is situated on the main line from Mons to Namur, about half-way between the two towns, and is about fifty miles directly south of Brussels, and roughly twenty-five miles from the French frontier.

LIEGE.—A city of Belgium, capital of the province of Liége, on the Meuse, on the influx of the Ourthe; 54 miles east by south of Brussels. It has a population of 243,800 and is the centre of the coalmining industry of the province. An international exhibition was held in 1905, but resulted in financial failure. Liége is famous for its University (founded in 1816); the library of which contains a quarter of a million volumes. It was strongly fortified by General de Brialmont and, under the command of General Leman, made a stout resistance against the Germans, whose first attacks were repulsed with great loss. General Leman was captured in Fort Loncin after it had been destroyed by artillery fire and while he was himself rendered unconscious by the fumes of exploded shells.

MAASTRICHT.—Town of the Netherlands, capital of the Dutch portion of the Province of Limburg, on the left bank of the Meuse, 56 miles east of Brussels and 52 miles west by south of Cologne. It has a population of 38,000, and among the industries carried on are the manufacture of earthenware, glass and crystal, arms and paper, as well as breweries and tobacco and cigar factories. Maastricht was formerly an important fortress. It was besieged by the Spaniards in 1576 and 1579 and taken by the French in 1673, 1748, and 1794. It is still considered a garrison town, but its ramparts were dismantled in 1871-1878. The church of St. Servatius is said to have been founded in the sixth century, thus being the oldest church in Holland.

MAUBEUGE.—A strongly-fortified town of France, in the Department of the Nord, on the Somme, 11 miles north of Avesnes, 13 miles south of Mons. It has a population of 23,200. It has an arsenal and manufactures glass. In 1793 the town was invested by the Prince of Saxe-Coburg, but it was relieved by the battle of Wattignies.

Maubeuge surrendered to the Germans, after being severely bombarded, on September 7.

MONS.—Situated about forty miles west of Namur, and about 140 miles from Paris. It is the centre of the chief coal-mining district of Belgium, and is an important railway junction, being the point at which two lines branch to Paris from the north. The eastern, or more direct line, is via Maubeuge, and is 155 miles to Paris, while the western route, via Douai and Arras, is 176 miles. Mons is situated on a hill and has been fortified for the past six centuries; it is connected by rail with Charleroi, thirty-five miles distant, and with Brussels, about forty-five miles away.

NAMUR.—A strongly fortified city of Belgium, capital of the province of the same name, at the confluence of the Sambre and the

Meuse, 36 miles south-east of Brussels. It has a population of 32,400, and the chief industry is the manufacture of cutlery. The Cathedral was built in 1751-67 from the designs of Pizzoni, of Milan. Namur was captured by Louis XIV. in 1692, by William III. in 1695, and again by the French in 1701, 1746, and 1792.

It was reported on August 24 that the city had been captured by the Germans, after a short siege.

SAMBRE.—A river of Northern France and Southern Belgium, rising in the valley which lies between the towns of Maubeuge and Guise in the north of France (Department Nord). It flows north-east by the town of Maubeuge, after which it turns more directly east, crosses the Belgian frontier, and continues a fairly straight course to Charleroi, whence it flows by many curves and convolutions to Namur, where it joins the River Meuse, which, later on, becomes the Maas in Dutch territory.

VALENCIENNES.—Situated on the right bank of the River Scheldt, about 157 miles north of Paris on the Paris-Brussels railway, at the point where the Schonelle and Scheldt join. It is the centre of an extensive and rich coalfield, and is largely engaged in iron and steel industries. Its population is upwards of 25,000. It is connected by rail with Lille and Maubeuge, as well as with various other centres, and is one of the most important towns of the Department of Nord. The Belgian frontier is about eight miles distant from the town. The lace for which Valenciennes used to be famed is but little made here now.

CPSIA information can be obtained at www.ICGtesting.com
Printed in the USA
LVOW03s1649160314

377625LV00020B/942/P

9 781277 469820